LINCOLN CHRISTIAN COLLEGE AND SEMINARY
P9-DEF-020

Beyond the Ordinary

BEYOND THE ORDINARY: TEN STRENGTHS OF U.S. CONGREGATIONS

By Cynthia Woolever and Deborah Bruce

Westminster John Knox Press
LOUISVILLE • LONDON

© 2004 Presbyterian Church (U.S.A.), A Corporation

All rights reserved. No part of this book may be reproduced or transmitted in any form or by any means, electronic or mechanical, including photocopying, recording, or by any information storage or retrieval system, without permission in writing from the publisher. For information, address Westminster John Knox Press, 100 Witherspoon Street, Louisville, Kentucky 40202-1396.

Book design by PerfecType, Nashville, Tennessee
Cartoons: © *copyright Chris Morgan, cxmedia.com. Cartoons in chapters 1, 2, 5, and 8 first printed in* Why People Don't Go to Church, *Open Book, 2002; cartoon in chapter 6 first printed in* Build My Church, *Open Book, 1999; cartoon in chapter 9 first printed in* Shaping the Future, *Open Book, 1997.*
Cover design by Mark Abrams

First edition
Published by Westminster John Knox Press
Louisville, Kentucky

This book is printed on acid-free paper that meets the American National Standards Institute Z39.48 standard. ♾

PRINTED IN THE UNITED STATES OF AMERICA

04 05 06 07 08 09 10 11 12 13 — 10 9 8 7 6 5 4 3 2 1

Library of Congress Cataloging-in-Publication Data

Woolever, Cynthia.
Beyond the ordinary : ten strengths of U.S. congregations / by Cynthia Woolever and Deborah Bruce.— 1st ed.
        p. cm.
      Includes bibliographical references.
      ISBN 0-664-22693-0 (alk. paper)
      1. Parishes—United States. I. Bruce, Deborah. II. Title.

    BV700.W65 2004
    250'.973—dc22

                                                                                2003057690

CONTENTS

108209

ILLUSTRATIONS

ACKNOWLEDGMENTS

WE GIVE SPECIAL THANKS . . .

To our current and former colleagues in Research Services, Presbyterian Church (U.S.A.): Keith Wulff (coordinator), Charlene Briggs, Rebecca Farnham, Charisse LeMaster, John P. Marcum, Amy Noh, Laura Oates, David Prince, Ida Smith-Williams, Janice Spang, and Jamie Spence.

To our colleagues who served as consultants: Robert Dixon, Trey Hammond, and Herb Miller.

To our colleagues who directed the Leader study: Jackson Carroll and Becky McMillan, the Pulpit & Pew Project of the Ormond Center, Duke University.

To other colleagues who supported the project: Steve Boots, Kenneth Byerly, Michael Cieslak, Ann Diebert, Carl Dudley, David Knoke, and David Roozen.

To our research colleagues who directed the denominational oversamples: Roger Dudley, Bryan Froehle, Mary Gautier, Kirk Hadaway, Richard Houseal, Phil Jones, Matthew Price, Marty Smith, and Craig This.

To our funding organizations and their officers: Chris Coble and John Wimmer, of Lilly Endowment Inc., and James Lewis, of the Louisville Institute.

And, most important, to the worshipers and their congregations who generously gave their time to help us portray extraordinary congregations.

©hris Morgan 2003

cxmedia.com

ORDINARY OR EXTRAORDINARY?

A farm, a tornado, a girl, her dog, and three friends following a yellow brick road: Frank Baum builds on common, familiar images to tell his fairy-tale adventure, *The Wonderful Wizard of Oz*. Baum's morality tale about the qualities needed to make it in the world says the trip requires brains, heart, and courage.[1]

Baum's characters—the Scarecrow, the Tin Woodman, and the Cowardly Lion—were fanciful but intentional ways of framing his message. These three characters symbolize the universal human qualities of mind, heart, and courage.[2] Congregations possess these same three qualities.

- *Every congregation has a mind.* What do we see inside our congregation and from our doors? Through our intelligence and thinking, what do we understand that view to mean?

- *Every congregation has a heart.* What do we feel about what we see? What gives us joy? For what do we grieve? From these feelings, what do we hope to imagine and create?

- *Every congregation has courage.* What will we do with what we see, feel, and imagine? What will we courageously seek, knowing there is no assurance of success?

In these pages we invite you to (1) discover the qualities that are evident in strong congregations—those that courageously use their minds and heart, (2) feel the dimensions and intensity of these qualities in strong congregations, and (3) have courageous conversations about what God calls congregations to do.[3]

A Language of Strengths

A recent edition of the *Ethnologue* lists "7,202 languages spoken worldwide, 440 of them within a generation or two of extinction."[4] The languages with which people describe "healthy congregations" and the definitions they use may not number in the thousands, but they certainly exceed several dozen. The various definitions derive at least in part from the definers and their different points of view. Based on theological agendas that are seldom inclusive, these lists of congregational health characteristics attract devoted followers. Our research moves leaders and people of faith beyond that definitional Tower of Babel toward a more comprehensive and useful language based on congregational strengths.

What is different about our approach? In much scientific research, studies examining weakness dominate the agenda, outdistancing efforts to comprehend the strengths of individuals or organizations. Martin Seligman, a former president of the American Psychological Association, critiqued his own discipline: "Psychology is half-baked, literally. We have baked the part about mental illness. We have baked the part about repair and damage. But the other side is unbaked. The side of strengths, the side of what we are good at, the side . . . of what makes life worth living."[5]

Seligman's colleagues and others apparently agree. During the 1990s, scientific journals published about a hundred studies on sadness for every one study on happiness. Now, a "positive psychology" movement emphasizing people's strengths and talents instead of their weaknesses is burgeoning.[6] We believe this shift in emphasis is also essential for understanding congregations. Grasping what makes congregations strong is more helpful than identifying organizational weaknesses.

What makes a congregation smart, imaginative, and courageous? The answer exposes much about our assumptions regarding congregations, our research strategies, and advice we might offer to help congregations. Describing a strong congregation rests on our understanding of what a congregation is and its purpose or mission.

An often-cited definition of a congregation, penned by James Hopewell,[7] says a congregation is a local organization in which people "regularly gather for what they feel to be religious purposes." This gathering of people has "a special name and recognized members who assemble regularly to celebrate a more universally practiced worship." But Hopewell insightfully notes that while these groups of people are tied to theology and activities practiced in other locations, each group has a local "story." Because people gather and communicate regularly, they develop distinct ways of practicing their faith (e.g., "this is how we do it here"); their own language; and their own way of seeing their past, present, and future. The popularity of this definition stems from its ability to capture the dual essence of congregational life: part universal and part local or unique.

Other universals related to purpose and mission help us describe and define congregations. First, congregations create spaces and places for emotional bonding. Congregations are communities in a tangible way. Worshipers who describe their congregation as family express this aspect of congregational life—the inclusive, often social activities of the congregation that help participants build strong ties to one another. People feel like they belong, have friends, and play an important role in the lives of others there. Second, congregations universally seek to educate worshipers about the faith and the behaviors expected of the faithful. Educational efforts aimed especially at the young may extend to starting schools where secular and religious education coincide.

Third, worshipers wish to share with others the faith and beliefs that are most meaningful to them. Congregations also seek new people to join their community of faith. Leaders and members recognize that, without new members to replace those who leave or die, the congregation has a finite future. Fourth, congregations of all faiths serve others, both within and outside their group. Serving behaviors come from a variety of theologies and worldviews, but helping others is one way all congregations seek to witness to the world. Fifth, and many would say most important, congregations convey to their worshipers and others that life has ultimate meaning. The day-to-day lives of worshipers and the mission of the congregation speak to something that transcends today's realities and challenges.

Using Our Brains

Evaluating a congregation's strengths should reflect how well it accomplishes those universals for which congregations exist. How is it doing at "being" a congregation? Strong congregations consistently and effectively achieve the goals for which congregations exist. Are they gathering people for worship that is meaningful to those in their community? Are they teaching others—especially the young—about their faith? Do they provide places where people are emotionally and spiritually nurtured? Are they replacing members and welcoming new people? Are they sharing their abundance with others? Are they working for a more just society? Are they conveying a message of hope and meaning?

Evaluating congregations in this way is similar to evaluating any other type of voluntary organization. It is a rational, analytical, and organizational approach. Congregations achieving the rigorous criteria of strong organizational life meet the same standard of performance as other voluntary organizations. While it's essential for congregations to use their brains, we believe that understanding the special nature of congregations requires additional benchmarks.

Like other voluntary groups, congregations tend toward maintaining the organization as it currently functions. What factors predict the creative, resourceful, inventive, enterprising, and visionary actions of congregations? What predicts which congregations will marshal their resources to act in extraordinary ways?

Getting to the Heart of It

The hearts of congregations respond on a feeling, intuitive, or imaginative level rather than on a cognitive level. Imaginative congregations do not live solely on the level of rationality; they respond with an openness that transcends current realities. What does the description of congregations as imaginative have to do with strength, health, or vitality? Samuel Taylor Coleridge said that the "imagination dissolves, dissipates, in order to re-create. . . . It struggles to idealize and to unify. It is essentially vital."[8] Imagination—

seeing beyond the visible to envision something new—is also a hallmark of congregational vitality. Congregations that draw upon the resources of their "heart" as well as their "mind" are more likely to focus on a bold vision for the future.

What are some characteristics of congregations with a strong heart? They possess a clear, widely owned vision of the future, openness to new possibilities, and a consensus about their identity as future-directed. They thrive on empowering and inspiring leadership in all areas of congregational life. These congregations do not believe they have exclusive control to organize and manage the story of their congregation. They do not see themselves as the sole authors of their faith community's story. They know Who is the real author of their story.

> ## MYTH TRAPS
>
> *Myths are tempting assumptions about congregational life. Just as cheese lures a mouse, myths lure us to beliefs we want to be true. Believing myths is its own reward. Myths allow us to avoid change and permit us to use the same old methods to get the same old results. Myths immobilize and trap us in dead ends, blocking us from fully living out the answer to our most important question: What is God calling us to be and do as a congregation?*

Seeking Courage

Congregations need courage to face both the present and the future. Courage is the spirit to hold one's own in spite of doubt, uncertainty, fear, or extreme difficulties. Tenacity and determination mark the courageous congregation. What keeps congregations from acting with bravery and pluck? Fear, uncertainty, and risk prevent congregations from going down the difficult path that no other congregation can or will travel. Many times congregational leaders ask what is working well for another congregation. They hope to copy or franchise successful methods rather than adapting them to their situation or creating their own strategies. Such inquiries reflect limited awareness of and coping with their congregation's uniqueness. Facing the reality of their one-of-a-kind mission requires will and soul. The perception of risk is accurate. As one set of writers observed,

"Nature places a simple constraint on those who leave the flock to go their own way. They get eaten!"[9] Congregational nature avoids failure, yet going in a distinctive way moves a congregation to greater strength.

For congregations to reach beyond the ordinary requires integration of three qualities—mind, heart, and courage. Beyond-the-ordinary congregations use their mind—suggesting *intelligence* and *analysis*. Beyond-the-ordinary congregations use their heart or imagination—suggesting *beyond-the-obvious solutions*. Beyond-the-ordinary congregations use their courage—suggesting a *responsive identity* whose actions result from the integration of heart and mind.

Exclusive reliance on their congregational ego or perceived reality limits their capacity for a wider imagination and larger heart. Exclusive reliance on the wealth of the mind prevents congregations from noticing how God is approaching them and what God is asking them to do. Exclusive reliance on imagination or heart leads congregations toward a future that is out of touch with reality. Integration of the heart and mind requires courageous conversations and learning the language of strengths.

Playing to Strengths

Consultants, researchers, and religious leaders often search for the "trump card"—the one key factor they believe makes a difference in congregational vitality and explains much about how congregations work. A favorite trump card is size. Some believe that knowing the size of a congregation reveals its strengths and weaknesses. Small congregations are different from mid-size congregations, which are different from large congregations. Countless books, articles, essays, and consulting practices suggest why and how a congregation's size matters. Some experts even specialize in helping congregations become a new, predetermined size. But if we focus on strengths, does size tell us anything? Are there strengths that can be found in any congregation, regardless of size?

Another trump card commonly used to analyze congregations is worship style. Many congregations experiment with contemporary styles of music, less formal services, and a host of other revisions in an attempt to update or transform their worship experiences. Is the issue both style and content? How do these changes help congregations remain faithful communities that accomplish their fundamental goals and mission?

Still another popular trump card deals with leadership. This wisdom holds that if a congregation has the right leader, everything goes right. Without the right leader, everything goes wrong. The whole challenge revolves around finding the right leader at the right time; then the congregation arrives in the promised land. Much of the literature about healthy or vital congregations places enormous stock in this one factor. The appeal is obvious. How could a congregation be strong without a strong leader? But which comes first—a strong congregation or a strong leader? Perhaps strong congregations are particularly good at finding, attracting, or supporting effective leaders. How much do the key leader's character, characteristics, and charisma interplay with other aspects of congregational life?

Another one-answer approach to dissecting congregations entails focusing on the mission orientation of the congregation. Some writers make compelling arguments that congregations should focus on what really matters.[10] If they do, everything else falls into place. Congregations—like other organizations—craft vision and mission statements, hoping to propel themselves into the future with the right set of words immortalized on paper. Yet *knowing* the mission and *doing* the mission are two different things. What keeps a congregation, a company, or any organization from moving beyond good thinking to purposeful action?

A few analysts have begun to identify how elements of congregational life might support and reinforce one another. In one instance, congregations are urged to locate their "minimum factor" and work to improve it.[11] This is yet another version of the trump-card approach, based on the myth that fixing weaknesses makes everything right. Despite the best efforts to fix weaknesses, purposeful actions sometimes unravel. Based on undocumented social science research, this advice encourages congregations to look at what is off the mark in their collective life. This approach unintentionally disempowers a congregation in two ways: (1) The congregation focuses on some aspect of its system that may never become one of its strengths; and (2) The process names *one* aspect of congregational life as the trump card. Both of these primrose paths may further remove congregational stakeholders from the discernment or decision-making process that builds genuine muscle on their congregation's potential.

Congregational Strength Is Always Plural

All trump-card or one-answer approaches—those we have just outlined, as well as others, such as theology, context, and the congregation's age (e.g., a new church vs. a dinosauric one)—assume that one factor alone explains most of what makes a congregation work. Most people are drawn to a simple answer built on one idea. But like painting a landscape in nothing but shades of gray, approaching the study of congregations with one-answer tricks yields little for sound action. Just as lack of color diminishes our view, knowing one part of the answer is not the same as knowing the whole answer. A character in a recent novel puts this conceptual error in these images: "If the truth is a loaf of bread and you pick up a crumb, do you have the truth? If not the truth, then it is as worthless as a lie."[12]

Our collected information supplies a matchless moment to explore multiple factors and how they interact to determine the strengths of America's congregations. When we search for a multidimensional view of congregations in American life, the scene begins to shift. We see beyond shades of gray to full color, beyond a one-hue view to the big landscape, beyond a crumb to the full loaf of bread, and beyond an ordinary understanding of congregational life to uncommon insight.

The research findings unfolded in the following chapters tell how complicated congregational life is at the local level. Each of the more than 2,000 congregations in our study represents a one-of-a-kind puzzle. Think of each congregation as a separate jigsaw puzzle being assembled in a dark room. Raising the window shades just slightly sheds light on what pieces are in place for each congregation, how big the pieces are, and the overall picture created by each congregational jigsaw. Our analysis describes the general patterns of this amazing mosaic of shape and color. And every congregation can assemble its unique puzzle from the multicolored, large and small pieces that represent its strengths.

A Data-Based Approach

Most studies of congregational life either take a case-study approach—viewing a small number of congregations at a time—or rely on the views of one person—the minister, pastor, priest, rabbi, or other key leader. Our picture is unique.

The immense scope of the U.S. Congregational Life Survey overcomes the limitations of drawing data from a few geographical locations or too few individuals within each congregation. More than 300,000 worshipers in over 2,000 congregations (randomly selected from throughout the United States) provide the most representative profile of worshipers and their congregations ever developed in the United States. Everyone fifteen years of age or older in religious services in the participating congregations responded to the questions by filling out a survey in April 2001. This scientific, national random sample of worshipers and their congregations offers a new opportunity to explore congregational life (see appendix 1 for more details).

Building on our previous work that describes worshipers and their characteristics,[13] our focus now broadens. Our purpose here shifts from the detailed and specific analysis of individual worshipers to profiles of congregations. We ask, "What are the qualities of a strong congregation?" rather than "What are the qualities of a faithful worshiper?" How do small congregations differ from large ones? What factors mutually relate to reinforce congregational strengths and vitality? How do congregations build a strong identity based on clear thinking and creative approaches to current realities?

Obscuring or revealing their distinctive strengths, congregations operate out of mental maps based on a complex mix of their hearts and minds. How accurate is the mental map we have of our congregation? How much of what we assume about congregations reflects the real ebb and flow of their lives? One writer asserts, "The map in our minds is much less a chart to our future than it is a description of our present limitations."[14] How limiting is our present map for the calling of our congregation?

Rather than relying on only one congregational strength, we found ten areas of strength in American congregations. Each of these ten strengths makes a congregation stand tall—placing it in the upper 20% of strength and effectiveness. We detail these ten vital strengths in subsequent chapters: (1) spirituality and faith development, (2) meaningful worship services, (3) participation in congregational activities, (4) a sense of belonging to the congregation, (5) caring for children and youth in the congregation, (6) community involvement, (7) sharing faith with others, (8) welcoming new people, (9) empowering congregational leadership, and (10) a vision for the congregation's future. All of these strengths contribute to the overall vitality and health of the congregation (see appendix 2 for measurement details).

Seeing the Whole Picture

A number of dynamics influence congregational decision making. Some decision-making factors arise from the congregation's mind—analysis of new information, reality-based reasoning, and our understanding of how things work in our faith community. Some of these factors come from the congregation's heart—what we passionately believe, our theology, biblical understandings or revelations from other sacred texts, traditions that create continuity and meaning, and prayer or discernment. Other decisions are based on courage—the belief that we can do extraordinary things and the willingness to take on difficult challenges. Unfortunately, many congregations rely exclusively on the realm of their mind or heart. Or if congregational leaders rely exclusively on their courage, their actions may be reckless, irrational, or unimaginative.

Dorothy needed all three of her friends to find her way first to Oz and eventually to her home in Kansas. While they walked the same road, their cooperation and reliance on their individual strengths meant they reached their goal. Each contribution—wisdom, heart, and courage—was equally important. Congregations drawing on their mind, heart, and courage will likewise move closer to their ultimate mission.

Do You Have What It Takes?

The Wonderful Wizard of Oz characters were not seeking wealth or fame but the life-altering qualities of wisdom, heart, and courage. At the end of the story, the Scarecrow, the Cowardly Lion, and the Tin Woodman learn that the Wizard is not a wizard at all but "a common man."[15] How will they find brains, heart, and courage? The Wizard informs them that they already possess what they desire. He points out the many ways the Scarecrow has been a thoughtful problem-solver, the Tin Woodman a compassionate friend, and the Lion a brave leader. He helps them see who they already *are*. Knowing themselves gives them confidence to face the future.

We contend that congregations already have or can obtain everything they need to transform their futures, because God has already given it. Like Dorothy who discovered she already had all the good life had to offer, including loving people around her, we often don't see the obvious. Can we move beyond our mental maps to see the possibilities for our congregation by building on its strengths?

Likewise, the following pages point to the ways congregations are already strong. By combining new knowledge and passionate hearts, they can journey toward fully embracing their calling.

©hris Morgan   2002

cxmedia.com

CHAPTER 1

STRENGTH 1:
GROWING SPIRITUALLY

There is one great difficulty with a good hypothesis. . . . [I]t is likely to become a thing in itself, a work of art. It is then like a finished sonnet or a painting completed. One hates to disturb it.[1]

JOHN STEINBECK

Hypothesis is another word for a good guess. Scientific analysis always begins with a good hypothesis to guide the study. But the end goal of the investigation is to draw conclusions or "answers" consistent with the facts. We hope the facts support the hypothesis, but that doesn't always happen. John Steinbeck shares his frustration with untested beliefs that are difficult to dislodge despite evidence to the contrary. He cites a humorous example of a "learned institution" that "extincted" sea otters. Even after the animals were photographed, the learned institution stuck to its original finding.

Steinbeck concludes, "When a hypothesis is deeply accepted it becomes a growth which only a kind of surgery can amputate." He says even after the so-called "facts" that created the beliefs are shown to be inaccurate, the beliefs may persist. And the practices stemming from these same beliefs have a life of their own. Too often the practices continue even when no one remembers the original beliefs.

Is surgery required to remove some of our beliefs about congregational life? Or could a simple "shot in the arm" of factual information help us better understand congregations? Most important, would we alter our practices because of this new information?

One of our most cherished beliefs is that strong congregations are built on the spiritual lives of their worshipers. And nearly everyone believes the spiritual dimension of congregations should be the most important strength of faith communities. This chapter presents new information about the part spirituality plays in congregations.

What Is a Strength?

A congregational strength, one aspect of any organization's dynamics, consistently operates, whether or not the worshipers or leaders are aware of it. Further, a real strength is imbedded in the behaviors, beliefs, and values of the majority of the worshipers. As a result, a number of worshipers can leave without diminishing this strength. A real congregational strength does not depend on a few key leaders. Congregational strengths gain momentum and muscle when they become central to the conscious identity of the congregation. Awareness of their congregational strengths brings joy and fulfillment to people in the congregation. Finally, we believe the most effective way for congregations to accomplish their important mission requires leveraging and building on their strengths.

What Is a Strong Congregation?

All congregations are strong, in different ways. All congregations possess some strengths. How can we make such a claim? This assertion rests on several assumptions we have about congregations. First, all congregations have strengths because in every congregation something works. The more congregations focus on what is working and use their strengths effectively, the stronger they become. Second, much of whatever congregations need more of already exists internally. Congregations become stronger when they search for solutions that are based on their current strengths. Third, all congregations have something of value from their past that can be used to carry them into a more positive future. Valuing and building on the past does not mean blind and undeviating allegiance to past practices or "bronzing" some aspect of earlier glory days. Congregations that honor the best of the past in making changes for the future have an "envisioned future grounded in the reality of the actual past."[2] These three assumptions describe the dynamics of all congregations.

What Is a Beyond-the-Ordinary Congregation?

Beyond-the-ordinary congregations embrace the three assumptions we described and reach a level of excellence in one or more areas of congregational life. Extraordinary congregations are not without weaknesses or problems because "excellence does not require perfection."[3] Through careful analysis of more than 2,000 congregations of all sizes and faith groups, we identified ten congregational strengths. If a congregation scores in the top half on any one of the ten indices, they are "above average" in that area of their ministry. If a congregation scores in the top 20% on any one or more of the ten indices, they are "beyond the ordinary" in that ministry area.

Finding Strength in Typical Congregations

The first strength we'll examine details the various spiritual climates we found in congregations—small or large, rural or urban, numerically growing or declining. Many congregations emphasize the spiritual development of their worshipers and participants. Yet while congregations may view this as a worthwhile goal, not all congregations have this strength on which to build more effective ministry. One almost sacred hypothesis held by congregational leaders is that "spiritually alive" congregations are also the strongest or fastest-growing congregations.[4] Is it true? Do the deepening spiritual lives of worshipers act as basic building blocks for strong congregations?

Five factors emerged as important elements reflecting the spiritual strengths among a national random sample of congregations. Figure 1.1 shows the percentage of worshipers in the *average* congregation who reported each element of this strength. Of the five elements, one stands out as a particular asset in most congregations in the United States—a large majority of worshipers in the average congregation (84%) feel their spiritual needs are being met within their congregation. This element is a general measure of satisfaction with the congregation's worship services and other activities offered by the congregation. The second element typical of U.S. congregations is worshipers' involvement in private devotional activities—72% of worshipers in the average congregation spend time in private devotions at least a few times a week. Another element is reported less often by American worshipers—less than half of worshipers have grown in their faith in the last year through congregational activities (43%). Finally, in the important arena of values, only one in five worshipers say the congregation's Bible study and prayer groups is what they most value about their congregation (21%), and fewer than one in six say the prayer ministry of the congregation is what they value most (16%).

These broad findings about the spiritual strength of typical congregations say cur-

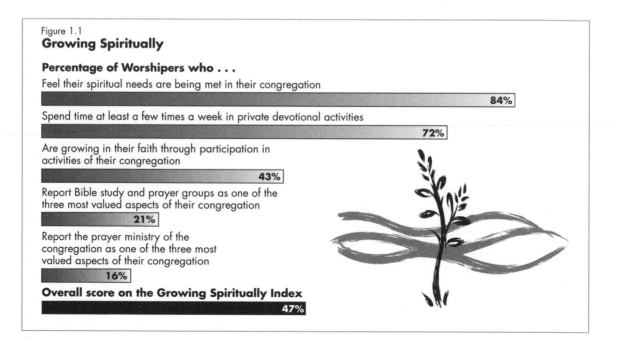

Figure 1.1
Growing Spiritually

Percentage of Worshipers who . . .

Feel their spiritual needs are being met in their congregation

84%

Spend time at least a few times a week in private devotional activities

72%

Are growing in their faith through participation in activities of their congregation

43%

Report Bible study and prayer groups as one of the three most valued aspects of their congregation

21%

Report the prayer ministry of the congregation as one of the three most valued aspects of their congregation

16%

Overall score on the Growing Spiritually Index

47%

rent attendees are highly satisfied with the worship services of their congregation. But the majority of worshipers are not experiencing significant growth in their faith primarily because of the worship services and other activities offered by the congregation. Three in four worshipers report pursuing spiritual growth through their private devotional activities. Further, the typical congregation cannot boast that activities like Bible study and prayer groups or prayer ministry are most highly valued by their worshipers relative to other aspects of their congregation. Keep in mind that these descriptions are of the *typical* congregation. Your congregation or another congregation may have a different set of strengths.

The Growing Spiritually Index

Through careful data analysis we determined that the five factors presented in Figure 1.1 are the key survey items that most accurately capture congregational spiritual vitality. These five facets taken together form an index, or composite snapshot, of the spiritual strength of a congregation. In contrast to a real thermometer, the "spiritual temperature" of congregations ranges from 0 to 100. The *typical* congregation has a spiritual temperature, or strength score, of 47% on the Growing Spiritually Index. Of course, we wouldn't expect any congregation to score a perfect 100% on this index. Nor is it likely for a congregation to

MYTH TRAP #1

Worshipers grow spiritually more through their own private devotional activities than through attending worship services.

In fact, both are important spiritual-growth behaviors and the two reinforce each other. In the typical congregation, three out of four worshipers spend time in private devotional activities. And four out of five worshipers attend services weekly. Congregations offering beyond-the-ordinary worship services also have a high percentage of worshipers who devote time to private prayer, study, and reflection on their faith. And beyond-the-ordinary congregations where many worshipers regularly devote time to private devotional activities are likely to offer extraordinary worship experiences as well.

completely fail with a temperature of 0! All congregations fall somewhere between these two extremes.

You might ask yourself: "Do all congregations do about the same in this area?" The answer is yes and no. While congregations vary in how well they are fostering the spiritual growth of their worshipers, we expected the differences to be larger. Most congregations fall within 11 percentage points on either side of the average score of 47%.[5]

Beyond-the-Ordinary Congregations

A score of 56% or above on the Growing Spiritually strength "thermometer" places a congregation in the top 20% of all congregations, an indication of being a "beyond-the-ordinary" or an above-average congregation. So, what do we know about congregations that are beyond the ordinary on the Growing Spiritually strength? Comparing congregations in the top 20% on the index to the 80% of congregations scoring below the "strength benchmark" (i.e., a score of 56%) lets us identify factors that distinguish between these two groups. Our statistical method forecasts which congregations fall in the extraordinary, or beyond-the-ordinary, group.[6]

Why look at extraordinary congregations rather than the average congregation? Making decisions based on what is true for the average person, situation, or organization is subject to the "illusion of averages."[7] The illusion refers to the blurry picture created by lumping two extreme groups—those from the top and those from the bottom—into one general box. This image cannot be sharpened because discovering what predicts the "average" doesn't identify the distinctive factors related to the highest 20% and the lowest 20%. Surely, more can be learned about what fosters excellence from the best 20% of any group—employees, customers, companies, or organizations—than by looking at what predicts average performance. The important question for us is what specific elements distinguish congregations rising to the top, or extraordinary, group.

Beyond-the-ordinary congregations—those possessing Growing Spiritually as a strength—typically have other strengths in their profile as well. A unique set of factors is responsible for putting congregations "over the top" in terms of spiritual vitality.

We found that most beyond-the-ordinary spiritually vital congregations possess four other strengths:

1. A strong sense of belonging to the congregation (Strength 4)

2. Meaningful worship (Strength 2)

3. High levels of worshiper participation in congregational activities (Strength 3)

4. Many new worshipers (Strength 8)

Congregations seeking to raise their spiritual "temperatures" can carefully review these related strengths to discover other ways to warm up to a new level of strength on the Growing Spiritually Index. In the conclusion, we summarize the factors that predict whether congregations score in the top 20% on each of the ten strengths (see Figure 11.2).

Does Congregational Size Matter?

Many congregations imagine their size, location, theology, context, or something else makes them unique and therefore exempt from these findings. Statements like "We're small," "We're liberal," "We're a new congregation," "We're all old people," "We're committed to community ministries," "We're invested in global causes," or "We're mostly 'seekers'" reflect attempts to hedge on why a congregation doesn't need to focus on a particular strength. One of the most-often used hedges is about size. Do small, mid-size, and large congregations differ in their spiritual strength? Yes, they do.

On four out of the five elements comprising the Growing Spiritually Index, small congregations (those with an average of fewer than 100 in worship) achieve *higher* scores than mid-size (between 100 and 350 in worship) and large congregations (more than 350 in worship). For example, small congregations are more likely to assist worshipers in their spiritual growth through congregational activities than are mid-size or large congregations. The differences by size of the congregation are too large to have occurred by chance. Yet on the remaining factor—worshipers reporting their spiritual needs are being

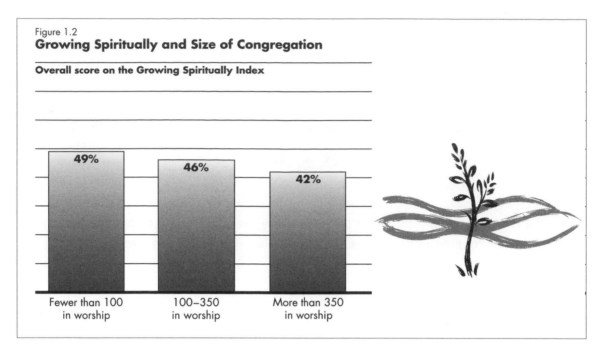

Figure 1.2

Growing Spiritually and Size of Congregation

Overall score on the Growing Spiritually Index

49%	46%	42%
Fewer than 100 in worship	100–350 in worship	More than 350 in worship

met—mid-size and large congregations are stronger. Worshipers in mid-size and large congregations are more satisfied with the spiritual nurture they receive from their congregation than those attending small congregations.

On the composite Growing Spiritually Index, as well, small congregations come out on top (see Figure 1.2). These findings lead to one conclusion—small congregations tend to be spiritually stronger than other congregations. In this area of congregational life (spiritual growth), small congregations have an advantage. Pound for pound, small congregations carry a lot of spiritual weight!

Does Congregational Theology Matter?

We also examined the relationship between denominational theology or religious beliefs and the Growing Spiritually Index. To look at this relationship, we grouped congregations into denominational families as a proxy for assessing worshipers' theology and beliefs directly (see appendix 3). Five categories captured the theological differences among congregations: Catholic parishes, mainline and liberal Protestant congregations, conservative Protestant congregations, congregations in historically black denominations, and other congregations (e.g., Mormon, Buddhist, other non-Christian). Because of the small number and considerable diversity of congregations in the "other" category, it was inappropriate to compare them as a group to the first four group categories. Therefore, we omitted the "other" category from the figures on differences between faith groups.

Does the theology of the congregation, represented by these broad groupings, affect the spiritual temperature of the congregation? Yes, it does. Conservative Protestant congregations and churches in historically black denominations consistently scored highest on the Growing Spiritually Index. This was true for all of the individual elements as well as for the composite index (see Figure 1.3). Mainline and liberal Protestant churches usually scored in the middle range. Catholic parishes made the lowest score on the index and its elements, with one exception—the meeting of spiritual needs. In this instance,

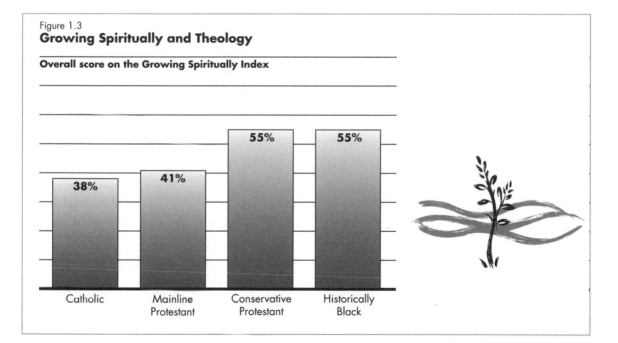

Figure 1.3
Growing Spiritually and Theology

Overall score on the Growing Spiritually Index

Catholic	Mainline Protestant	Conservative Protestant	Historically Black
38%	41%	55%	55%

WHAT MATTERS FOR GROWING SPIRITUALLY?		WHO EXCELS?
Congregational size . . . . Yes	→	Small congregations
Theology Yes	→	Conservative Protestant and historically black denomination churches
Age profile of worshipers . . . . . . No		
Negative predictor of numerical growth		

Catholic parishes had slightly higher marks, indicating their worshipers were more highly satisfied with the parishes' ability to meet their spiritual needs than those in mainline Protestant churches. But both are still below the average score of conservative Protestant congregations.[8]

These findings show the theology, beliefs, and religious practices stressed by congregations in two traditions—conservative Protestants and churches from historically black denominations—are linked to positive spiritual climates. Congregations in other faith families are challenged to examine and learn from the ways these congregations foster spiritual growth.

What Else Matters?

What about other situations or factors that might affect the spiritual temperature of the congregation, such as the age and gender profile of the membership, or the community around the congregation?

Considerable research explores how the age profile of the congregation correlates with the values and behaviors of worshipers. We discovered that congregations with a younger age profile scored about the same on the Growing Spiritually Index as congregations with an older age profile.[9] Therefore, congregations can be spiritually vital with younger or older worshipers. The age profile of the worshipers is irrelevant for the presence of this congregational strength.

Finally, the context or community around the congregation is another important condition to consider when analyzing spiritual strength. However, exploring the community context requires more analysis than can be reported here and will be addressed in subsequent publications.

Will Growing Spiritually Help Us Grow in Numbers?

Congregations are a complex mix of many ingredients. When following a recipe to make an entrée, a chef must include every ingredient on the list or the end result will not taste as it should. Some ingredients have a significant taste on their own (e.g., salt), but their flavor may be overpowered when combined with other ingredients. However, if the chef left salt out of the mix of ingredients, the end result might taste flat or less flavorful. Similarly, many congregational strengths are important "spices" in the mix of ingredients explaining numerical growth. When you put all the strengths in the "mix," some become less important and others become more important for understanding numerical growth. Just as in a recipe, when other congregational factors are added, some strengths recede into the background. This does not mean they are irrelevant or unimportant. It simply means they are less powerful in directly predicting numerical growth.[10]

Is Growing Spiritually a critical or less important ingredient for understanding numerical growth? Our research indicates that congregations with high scores on the Growing Spiritually Index are *less* likely to be growing numerically. Obviously, this reverse relationship is not what we expected to find. High levels of spiritual growth among worshipers in congregations are a powerful predictor of *little* numerical growth. How could that be the case? Unfortunately, congregations that are strong in the area of spiritual growth are rarely strong in welcoming new people, a congregational strength that powerfully predicts growing in numbers. But just because this tends to be the case currently does not mean it *should* be that way or will always be that way in the future. And it is not true for *every* congregation. Our analysis points to the importance of a "mix" of congregational strengths rather than a focus on one or two key factors.

Why Growing Spiritually Matters

How well did we do on this hypothesis: The spiritual dimension of congregational life is one of the most important strengths of faith communities? Some American congregations are not building on the strength of worshipers' spiritual growth. As Steinbeck warned, our *beliefs* matter because our behaviors and our practices stem from our beliefs. We cannot assume that every congregation enjoys a strong spiritual dimension. Yet, our belief about the prime role spirituality plays in congregational health persists even when the "facts" are suspect.

The following chapters reveal that spiritual vitality is foundational for strong congregations. Someone asked the poet Longfellow how he had achieved such a long and happy life. Pointing to an apple tree, Longfellow replied, "The secret of the apple tree is that it grows a little new wood each year. That's what I try to do."[11] Frederick Buechner echoes that conviction: "When faith stops changing and growing, it dies on its feet."[12] We believe congregations whose members fail to spiritually change and grow risk a similar fate.

THE MOST POPULAR FORM OF
ALTERNATIVE WORSHIP
AT ST PETER'S WAS
THE RAISING OF LEGS

CHAPTER 2

STRENGTH 2:
MEANINGFUL WORSHIP

[F]aith is closest to worship because, like worship, it is essentially a response to God.[1]

FREDERICK BUECHNER

Defining meaningful worship is as difficult as defining faith. How do current worshipers respond to what happens in services? What do they value about the worship services? How do the services relate to their everyday lives?

This chapter tests assumptions about what makes worship work. For example, some leaders believe that the size or the age profile of the congregation is strongly related to the vitality of congregations and meaningfulness of worship services. They believe that larger congregations with younger worshipers are more attractive to newcomers. If worshipers vote with their feet, does meaningful worship serve as a solid foundation on which strong congregations are built? If so, how is meaningful worship related to other strengths in the congregation?

Measuring Worship as Response

In our analysis we determined that eight factors capture the important qualities of meaningful worship. The eight qualities are shown in Figure 2.1 in rank order, from the highest percentage to the lowest percentage of worshipers expressing each opinion. In a typical congregation, at least three in four worshipers report they "always" or "usually" experience joy, inspiration, and God's presence during the worship services. The percentage of worshipers responding that the sermons, preaching, or homilies are one of the three most valued aspects of their congregations is 39%. This means almost one in five worshipers chose "preaching or homilies" as one of the top three aspects they *most* value about their congregation. In the typical congregation, preaching is second only to celebrating Holy Communion, the Eucharist, or the Lord's Supper in what people most value.[2]

Fortunately, most worshipers are not bored in services or frustrated by what they experience there. And attendees report that services are helpful to their everyday lives. What seems to be absent from congregations in the United States, however, is a "sense of awe." In the typical congregation, only one in four worshipers said they "always" or "usually" experience awe during worship.

Our findings reveal that congregations wishing to make their worship services more meaningful should look for ways to inspire, bring joy, help worshipers feel God's presence, and minimize boredom and frustration. Congregations can improve these five experiences through the style and content of music, the liturgy, the sermon or homily, the sacraments, and many other aspects of congregational worship. The results of this study do not dictate the particular *methods*, but they do point to the desired outcomes of worship elements.

The Meaningful Worship Index

The eight facets of congregational worship in Figure 2.1 form a second index or composite picture of a congregational strength—the Meaningful Worship Index. As with our first chapter's Growing Spiritually Index, congregations could score between 0% and 100% on the Meaningful Worship Index. And like before, all congregations fall in

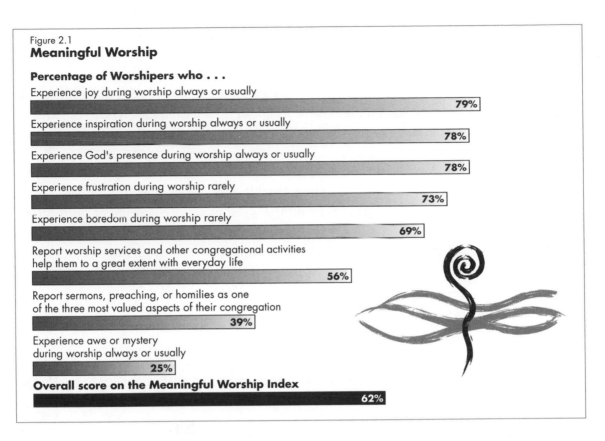

Figure 2.1
Meaningful Worship

Percentage of Worshipers who . . .

Experience joy during worship always or usually
79%

Experience inspiration during worship always or usually
78%

Experience God's presence during worship always or usually
78%

Experience frustration during worship rarely
73%

Experience boredom during worship rarely
69%

Report worship services and other congregational activities
help them to a great extent with everyday life
56%

Report sermons, preaching, or homilies as one
of the three most valued aspects of their congregation
39%

Experience awe or mystery
during worship always or usually
25%

Overall score on the Meaningful Worship Index
62%

between these two extreme scores. The typical congregation has a score of 62% on the Meaningful Worship Index. This score becomes significant only when we examine how much scores vary across congregations of different types.

Are all congregations doing equally well in providing meaningful worship? The answer to this question is similar to the answer in the previous chapter. While congregations vary in how well they're meeting the needs of worshipers through their services, the range is not large. Most congregations fall within about 11 percentage points on either side of the average score of 62%.[3]

It is important to remember that all of the findings reported in this chapter, as well as in the rest of the book, are based on the responses of people who were sitting in the pews on the day the survey was given. Most are regular worshipers who wouldn't attend if worship wasn't meeting their needs.[4] However, some people attend services in part out of a sense of obligation.[5] In the average congregation, two out of three people regularly feel a sense of meeting an obligation by attending worship services. Yet those who attend out of a sense of obligation also find worship services meaningful. Thus, regular worshipers attend because the services meet their needs at a level sufficient to ensure their return.

Unfortunately, we do not have a parallel Meaningful Worship Index score for people who are *not* currently attending worship services anywhere. Non-participants may have visited a congregation, found the worship services boring or uninspiring, and decided not to return. The scores in this area of congregational life are likely to be biased in a positive direction because the answers come from satisfied, returning "customers."

Beyond-the-Ordinary Congregations

What do we know about congregations that are beyond the ordinary on the strength of Meaningful Worship?[6] Two important factors emerged that push congregations to the top of the charts on the Meaningful Worship Index:

1. Worshipers who are growing spiritually (Strength 1)

2. Leadership that empowers lay involvement (Strength 9)

Congregations that wish to be stronger in the area of worship can review the dimensions of congregational life captured in these two other strengths. For example, encouraging worshipers' private devotional activities, one element of the Growing Spiritually Index, may help worshipers experience collective worship in a more positive and personally rewarding way. The reverse is also likely to be true. Worshipers who find the public experience of worship satisfying may be encouraged to pursue their spiritual growth through private devotions, prayer, or reading the Bible or other materials.

Congregational leaders in places where meaningful worship happens find ways to convey through the elements of the service (e.g., sermons or homilies, music, Holy Communion, or Eucharist) the message that every person of faith makes a one-of-a-kind contribution. Further, this kind of leadership inspires people to develop a faith that brings more meaning to their daily lives.

Does Congregational Size Matter?

A colleague who is familiar with our research asked us, "Where does God go?" His point was that if some congregations are more likely to report the presence of God—then God indeed must be present. This might be consistent with some theological views, but it may also be a consequence of worshipers' *expectations*. Perhaps some worshipers have a higher *expectation* of

MYTH TRAP #2

Large congregations offer the "best" worship experiences.

Meaningful worship happens in congregations of all sizes. All congregations hold services where people feel joy and inspiration. These congregational strengths do not depend on size. But what predicts beyond-the-ordinary performance on meaningful worship? Two factors matter: congregations that have empowering leaders and worshipers who are growing spiritually.

finding God or experiencing joy or feeling a sense of awe in worship. It is impossible to determine which of the above are "true." But our findings can shed some light on the experiences of worshipers in different contexts, even if our measurement rests on their subjective descriptions of those experiences.

Since the emergence of mega-churches and the often unique style and content of worship elements in such settings, many feel larger congregations have an advantage in putting together the "best" services. Is this true? Do worshipers in larger congregations experience more meaningful worship? The answer is no. Congregational size is not linked to the Meaningful Worship Index. *Meaningful worship happens in congregations of all sizes.*

Yet some of the individual facets that make up this index are related to congregational size. For example, in large congregations (those with more than 350 in attendance) more worshipers said they feel not only God's presence during worship but a sense of awe as well. However, in the typical small congregation (those with fewer than 100 in attendance) fewer worshipers experience boredom or frustration in worship than in mid-size or large congregations. Smaller congregations are also more likely than larger congregations to hold services that help worshipers with their everyday lives.

Does Congregational Theology Matter?

Yes, theology is related to how people experience worship. The relationship is probably indirect—religious beliefs and theology tend to influence which practices congregations exercise in worship. The rules or practices of what constitutes "worship" stem from the foundational beliefs a congregation has about what it means to be a people of faith. To explore the relationship of theology to meaningful worship, we used the same four denominational family categories presented in the first chapter.

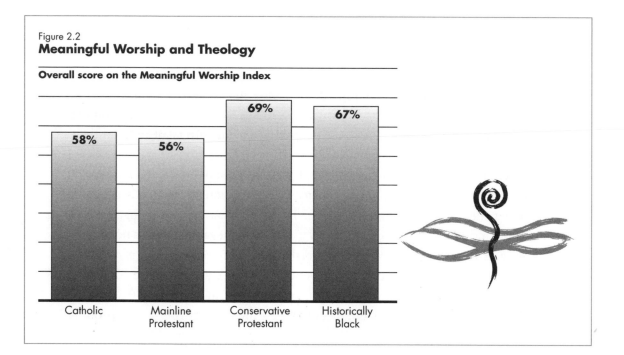

Figure 2.2
Meaningful Worship and Theology

Overall score on the Meaningful Worship Index

Catholic	Mainline Protestant	Conservative Protestant	Historically Black
58%	56%	69%	67%

Conservative Protestant and historically black churches consistently scored higher on the Meaningful Worship Index than Catholic parishes or mainline Protestant congregations (see Figure 2.2). Does this mean the worship services in conservative Protestant and historically black churches are actually *different* than services in the other two traditions? Or does it mean that *worshipers* in the conservative Protestant and historically black churches have different *expectations*? It is probably some of both. Also, expectations and actual experiences tend to coincide over the long run. If worshipers' experiences do not match their expectations, they probably won't continue to attend. What can we learn from the services of these two top-scoring traditions?

What Else Matters?

Current wisdom implies that the style of music and other features of worship either attract or repel younger worshipers. While we can't investigate this question directly with our study, we can compare how worshipers in congregations with different age profiles respond to their worship experiences. We found no differences between the congregations with younger age profiles and older age profiles on the Meaningful Worship Index. Congregations with younger worshipers and those with older worshipers satisfy those present equally well.

However, we found age-related differences on two of the elements of the index—experiencing boredom and the value placed on sermons or homilies. "Younger congregations," those where the average age of worshipers was younger than the typical congregation, have more reports of boredom. Younger congregations also place a higher value on the importance of sermons or homilies than "older congregations," those where the age profile was older than average.[7]

Will Meaningful Worship Help Us Grow in Numbers?

Congregations with high scores on the Meaningful Worship Index were *not* more likely to be growing in numbers of new people. Obviously, meaningful worship is an

Congregational size...........	No	
Theology	Yes →	Conservative Protestant and historically black denomination churches
Age profile of worshipers	No	

Not related to numerical growth

important part of any strong congregation.[8] So, what could explain the fact that meaningful worship does not lead to numerical growth? At least two possibilities exist. First, we found congregations were quite similar in how worshipers experienced worship. This simply means current worshipers are satisfied with the services or they would no longer be attending. Explaining small differences between congregations is far more difficult than explaining large differences. And because our index is a subjective measure based on how current worshipers feel, it doesn't tell us how a newcomer might experience worship services. Obviously, if a worship service is compelling to large numbers of people, current as well as potential attendees, it is more likely to draw in new people.

A second reason may explain the fact that meaningful worship does not predict numerical growth. As we discussed in the previous chapter, when the influence of other congregational characteristics is taken into account, some strengths recede into the background. Meaningful Worship is one of these strengths. This strength is less powerful in directly explaining numerical growth than other congregational strengths or factors (e.g., levels of participation in the congregation).

Why Meaningful Worship Matters

An older woman hoping to comfort her much younger friend about facing life's difficulties told her, "I was poor and unhappy until I was forty-five years old." Her younger friend sighed, "That's terrible. What happened next?" The older woman replied, "I got used to it."[9]

We found current attendees are highly satisfied with their congregation's worship services. But we also know that only 21% of Americans are sitting in the pews or gathering for worship during a typical week.[10] Current worshipers are used to their circumstances and can no longer see or feel as a new worshiper would. Low national average attendance levels challenge our tendency to make current participants happy while ignoring the yearning for meaningful worship by others in the community.

JASPER HAD A UNIQUE TALENT
OF WHISTLING THROUGH HIS EARS.

WHETHER OR NOT THIS WAS
A SPIRITUAL GIFT AND HOW IT COULD
BE USED FOR THE ADVANCEMENT
OF GOD'S KINGDOM REMAINS
THE SUBJECT OF BITTER DEBATE
AT HIS LOCAL CONGREGATION

©hris Morgan   2003   cxmedia.com

CHAPTER 3

STRENGTH 3: PARTICIPATING IN THE CONGREGATION

[W]hat church members find most compelling, what causes them to make the time for church in the context of a busy life, is the sense that they get something there that they get no where else.[1]

PENNY EDGELL

Being in a congregation involves "doing" something there. Attending worship services is typically the most common activity. But many of the faithful participate in congregational life via one or more additional avenues—by joining study or discussion groups; by assuming leadership in decision making; and by giving time, talent, and money in other ways.

Another hypothesis about congregational life suggests that strong congregations achieve a high percentage of "active" participants. Yet many leaders define "the time squeeze" as one of the most pressing issues facing their congregation today.[2] Edgell proposes that the "problem of time" misdirects our attention away from the importance of the choices people make. She asserts that congregations whose participants express and act out their religious values "generate commitment" and successfully compete for worshipers' time.

How are worshipers involved in their congregations? Does participation for some mean showing up for services a couple of times a year? Is it the same group of people who seem to do everything? Or is the load of leadership and financial support carried by a large number of people? This chapter explores what our data say about these important questions.

Just How Involved Is "Involved"?

This third strength, the level and type of worshiper participation, is best summarized by five factors showing the central ways people are involved in their congregations. Figure 3.1 shows the types of participation in rank order, from the ones worshipers are most likely to be doing to the ones they are least likely to be doing.

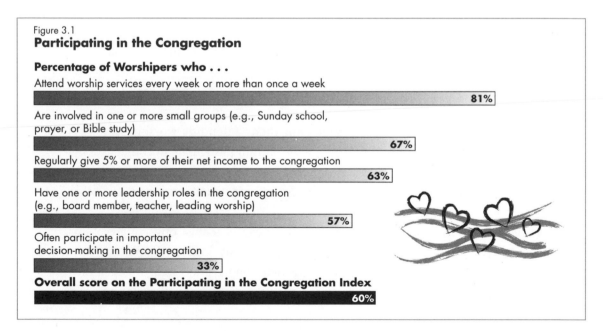

Figure 3.1
Participating in the Congregation

Percentage of Worshipers who . . .

Attend worship services every week or more than once a week
81%

Are involved in one or more small groups (e.g., Sunday school, prayer, or Bible study)
67%

Regularly give 5% or more of their net income to the congregation
63%

Have one or more leadership roles in the congregation (e.g., board member, teacher, leading worship)
57%

Often participate in important decision-making in the congregation
33%

Overall score on the Participating in the Congregation Index
60%

Regularly attending worship services is what the largest percentage of people do in the typical congregation. Four out of five people in the average congregation attend services weekly or more often. Beyond attending services, more people are involved in some type of group (e.g., discussion, Bible study) than anything else we asked about—approximately two in three participate in one or more of their congregation's groups. Slightly lower percentages—not quite two in three—regularly make more than minimal monetary contributions to their congregation. Slightly more than half of the average congregation's worshipers serve in some kind of leadership role. Finally, about a third of the people in a typical congregation take part in the decision-making process.

The Participating in the Congregation Index

These five types of participation form a third index—the Participating in the Congregation Index—a snapshot of the level of worshiper engagement in a congregation. The average congregation has a score of 60% on this index.

How much do congregations differ in terms of worshipers' involvement? Most congregations fall within about 13 percentage points of the average score of 60%. While this range is slightly larger than we saw for the congregational strengths of Growing Spiritually and Meaningful Worship, it is still not huge. Congregations tend to be alike in this area as well. The conclusion? Congregations are *far more alike* in terms of how many and in what ways people participate than they are different.[3]

Beyond-the-Ordinary Congregations

What do we know about beyond-the-ordinary congregations, those in the top 20% on the Participating in the Congregation Index? Congregations that enjoy high levels of worshiper involvement also tend to have three other strengths as well.[4] Their worshipers are more likely to:

1. Be growing spiritually (Strength 1)

2. Be inviting others to worship services and talking with others about their faith (Strength 7)

3. Share a strong vision for the congregation's future (Strength 10)

The Participating in the Congregation Index scores tell us a lot about what is happening in a congregation. The variety of other strengths tied to worshiper participation implies congregations should look closely at this strength. It is both influenced by several other areas and is probably reinforcing them as well. Strong congregations find their worshipers investing in the congregation in a number of ways—by their participation but also by inviting and welcoming others, seeking spiritual growth, and talking with others about their faith. Also, participation levels seem to rise when worshipers are engaged and excited by the future direction of the congregation.

MYTH TRAP #3

Congregations differ widely in their ability to involve large numbers of people in any activity other than attending worship services.

Actually, congregations exhibit fairly similar levels of worshiper participation. No congregation achieves 100% participation by all worshipers in all the offered activities and programs. Encouraging involvement that goes deeper than worship attendance challenges congregations equally. Beyond-the-ordinary congregations convey to worshipers the sense that spiritual growth stems from being a "player" rather than a "spectator."

Does Congregational Size Matter?

A congregation's size has a major impact on people's participation. But it's not that more people equals more participation. Size makes a difference in terms of *whether* and *how* people participate. The smallest congregations (those with fewer than 100 in worship) have the largest proportion of people participating (see Figure 3.2). Mid-size congregations typically have a *smaller* percentage of people participating in the congregation, and large congregations have the *lowest* percentage of all. These differences meet the statistical tests for significance—too large to have occurred by chance.

Not only do large congregations have the

lowest scores on the Participating in the Congregation Index, they also have the lowest scores on four of the five elements that make up the index. Large congregations typically have a smaller percentage of people involved in small groups, participating in decision making, assuming leadership positions, and regularly giving 5% or more of their income to the congregation. However, congregations of different sizes do not differ in the percentage of people who *regularly* attend worship services, though they are very different when it comes to other ways people are drawn deeper into the congregation.

Does Congregational Theology Matter?

Two traditions—conservative Protestants and historically black denominations—are quite *similar* in terms of how worshipers participate in their congregations. These two faith groups are quite *dissimilar* to what worshipers do in the two other traditions—Catholic

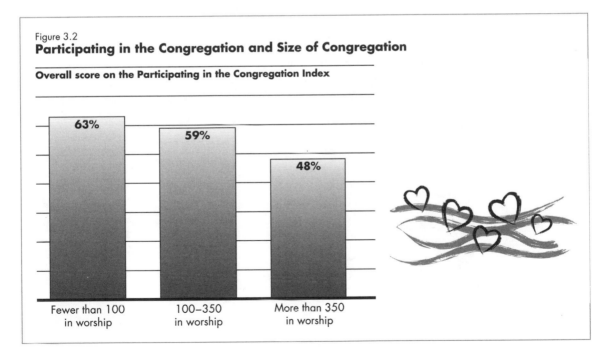

Figure 3.2
Participating in the Congregation and Size of Congregation

Overall score on the Participating in the Congregation Index

63% — Fewer than 100 in worship
59% — 100–350 in worship
48% — More than 350 in worship

parishes and mainline Protestant churches. Congregations in the latter two traditions have substantially lower participation rates than conservative Protestant and historically black churches (see Figure 3.3). In fact, Catholic parishes and mainline Protestant churches do not exhibit patterns of strong participation—their typical scores are *lower* than the national average for all congregations. In contrast, typical scores in conservative Protestant and historically black churches are *higher* than the national average.

Among the individual elements in the Participating in the Congregation Index, the scores follow a similar pattern with a few exceptions. Worship attendance rates are lowest for mainline Protestants but similar among the other three groups. Catholic parishes rise to the high attendance group with conservative Protestants and historically black denominations, probably as a result of the emphasis on weekly Mass attendance. Historically black denomination churches can claim the highest rates of participation in decision making.

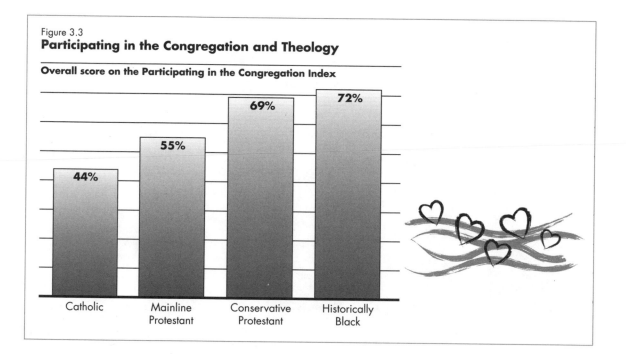

Figure 3.3
Participating in the Congregation and Theology

Overall score on the Participating in the Congregation Index

- Catholic: 44%
- Mainline Protestant: 55%
- Conservative Protestant: 69%
- Historically Black: 72%

Our findings point to the high levels of church participation among worshipers in two traditions (conservative Protestants and historically black denominations) and the fairly low levels in the other two traditions, Catholicism and mainline Protestant denominations. In short, worshipers are behaving differently in contexts that vary in beliefs, theology, and faith traditions.

What Else Matters?

The average age of people in the congregation is *not* related to the congregational strength of participation.[5] Congregations with older worshipers are just as likely to have high levels of worshiper involvement as congregations with younger worshipers. The reverse is also true. Congregations with a younger profile cannot take for granted that they will enjoy higher rates of worshiper involvement than congregations with much older members.

True or False: The 20% Rule

One of the untested assumptions about churches, parishes, and congregations is that 20% of the people carry the weight of the entire congregation. At the other extreme are a few people whose participation happens by sprinkling—water, rice, and dirt (at baptism, marriage, and burial). In between, a sizable percentage show up at worship but sit in the bleachers during other congregational activities.

Is it true that a small number of faithful people take care of most of the congregation's business? Is it the same people who come to all the activities, plan them, show up early to plug in the coffee pot, and stay late to clean up? Is this how it actually works in the average congregation, or does it just seem that way?

We tested this hypothesis by tabulating the five ways people participate in a congregation: (1) attending services; (2) joining a small group, such as Sunday school, discussion or study group, or Bible study or prayer group; (3) holding a leadership position; (4) being a part of congregational decision making; and (5) regularly giving money. In

WHAT MATTERS FOR PARTICIPATION?		WHO EXCELS?
Congregational size . . . . Yes	→	Small congregations
Theology Yes	→	Conservative Protestant and historically black denomination churches
Age profile of worshipers . . . . . . No		

Positive predictor of numerical growth

the average congregation, *one-third* of the worshipers participate in at least four of these ways. *Half* of all worshipers in the typical congregation participate in three or more ways.

The evidence doesn't match this "20% rule." Higher percentages of people in a typical congregation are participating and contributing to congregational life. Where do our perceptions about the overburdened few come from? The number and type of tasks required to keep an average congregation running smoothly stay about the same over a number of years. However, the number of people or the pool of volunteers available to handle these responsibilities has declined in many congregations due to membership loss. In most faith families, the majority of United States congregations are smaller in size than they were twenty years ago. Yet their decision making and operational structure may remain the same. These circumstances challenge congregations to refocus on the essentials of their basic mission in the world and to then identify the most effective and efficient strategies for meeting their central objectives.

Will Participating in the Congregation Help Us Grow in Numbers?

The Participating in the Congregation Index powerfully predicts numerical growth. Congregations grow in numbers when many people in the congregation engage in activities there. High levels of involvement continue to explain numerical growth even when the influence of other strengths and congregational factors (e.g., size) is taken into account. What is the central finding? While levels of involvement are important, this strength typically does not appear alone in a numerically growing congregation. A complex "mix" of ingredients makes up the recipe leading to numerical growth.[6]

Why Participating in the Congregation Matters

To argue quality over quantity is comforting when less is what you've got. Should leaders pay attention to low or declining participation? Should leaders be concerned that few worshipers are drawn into the life of the congregation beyond worship? Yes. The Participating in the Congregation Index is like a fishing bobber drifting on the water's surface. When the index stays the same or drifts, not much is happening beneath the surface. But when the congregation is strong, the bobber or the index says, "You've got something on the line!"

©hris Morgan 2003

cxmedia.com

CHAPTER 4

STRENGTH 4:
HAVING A SENSE OF BELONGING

When you are understood, you are at home. Friendship is the nature of God.[1]

JOHN O'DONOHUE

It's one thing to go somewhere and know you're welcome. It's another thing to arrive and feel like you're part of the family. So much of congregational life revolves around the closeness people feel as they worship together, experience life's joys and sorrows, and share their deepest values and beliefs. Strong congregations find ways to encourage emotional attachment while giving people the freedom to be themselves.

If an organization—whether it's a corporation, street gang, or congregation—provides people with love, a sense of belonging, and self-esteem, it will attract and retain new members. But any group that fails to meet these basic human needs finds "surviving and flourishing an elusive dream."[2] Do strong congregations, whatever their size, location, or theology, illustrate that principle? This chapter investigates whether these feelings are a weight-bearing wall in the structure of strong congregations.

The Importance of Feeling

The fourth congregational strength that emerged from our analysis is worshipers' sense of belonging and feeling attached to their congregation. Three questions addressed this area of congregational life: Do you feel like you belong and is that feeling growing? Do most of your close friends also attend here? Is your participation in the congregation growing, declining, or remaining about the same? While the three questions are closely linked, the *feeling* of belonging is fostered by close friendships. And increasing participation is probably an outcome of both close friendships and feeling at home. Certainly, declining involvement predicts less attachment in the future, as in some way the worshiper is already emotionally saying "good-bye."

The Having a Sense of Belonging Index

The three questions we just outlined are reflective of worshipers' sense of belonging to their congregations. The questions form a composite picture—the Having a Sense of Belonging Index. The typical congregation has a score of 36% on the index, which could range between 0% and 100% (see Figure 4.1).

Almost all congregations describe themselves as "friendly," "warm," and "welcom-

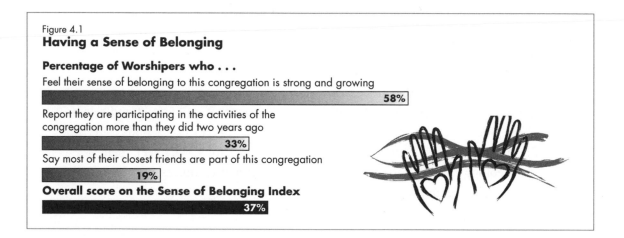

Figure 4.1
Having a Sense of Belonging

Percentage of Worshipers who . . .

Feel their sense of belonging to this congregation is strong and growing
58%

Report they are participating in the activities of the congregation more than they did two years ago
33%

Say most of their closest friends are part of this congregation
19%

Overall score on the Sense of Belonging Index
37%

ing." If these descriptions are true, congregations should have roughly the same scores on the Having a Sense of Belonging Index. And in fact, congregations' scores on the index are moderately similar. Scores on the index varied about 11 points on either side of the average of 36% percent.[3] Are congregations really friendly? Do they help people feel like they belong? You'd have to be there to know for sure. But these statistics imply that congregations are more alike on a "friendliness" scale than they are different.

Beyond-the-Ordinary Congregations

What kind of aerobic exercises increase congregational heart rates, placing congregations in the top 20% on the Having a Sense of Belonging Index?[4] Two other emotion-linked strengths foster excellence in a congregation's sense of belonging:

1. Congregations whose participants are growing spiritually (Strength 1)

2. Congregations possessing an imaginative vision for the future (Strength 10)

The first link says congregations that encourage spiritual growth and development are fostering emotional attachment to their place of worship as well. The second link says worshipers who are spiritually connected are also emotionally connected. Strong congregations capture worshipers' imaginations about the future of the congregation. In multiple ways strong congregations persuade their worshipers that the best years lie ahead. Feelings of belonging and imagining the future stem from a congregation's heart.

Twenty-five years ago Alvin Toffler asserted that a fulfilling emotional life is met through three basic requirements: "the need for community, structure, and meaning."[5] That assertion seems accurate today for beyond-the-ordinary congregations.

Does Congregational Size Matter?

Is it easier to feel like you belong in a small congregation than in a large one? The average scores on the Having a Sense of Belonging Index were highest in small congregations, slightly lower in mid-size congregations, and lowest in large congregations (see Figure

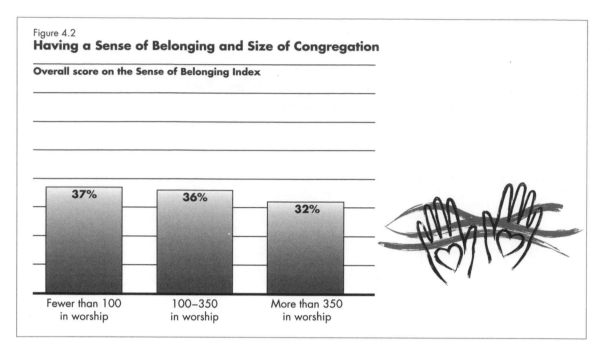

Figure 4.2
Having a Sense of Belonging and Size of Congregation

Overall score on the Sense of Belonging Index

37%	36%	32%
Fewer than 100 in worship	100–350 in worship	More than 350 in worship

4.2). Simply put, this means that worshipers in small congregations have a greater sense of belonging than participants in large congregations. This finding should challenge large congregations to do what they can to help people feel they are in the right place.

The size of the congregation doesn't make a difference in whether people have close friends within the congregation or whether their participation is increasing or decreasing. But small congregations do have a larger percentage of worshipers who say their sense of belonging is growing stronger.

Does Theology Matter?

The pattern we've seen in earlier indices of congregational strength repeats itself here (see Figure 4.3). Conservative Protestant and historically black churches typically have higher scores on the Sense of Belonging Index than the two other denominational groups—Catholic parishes and mainline Protestant congregations. Which comes first—a sense of belonging—or participation, spiritual growth, and meaningful worship? It is impossible to determine what is cause and what is effect. But a strong sense of belonging is a fourth link in the chain of strengths characteristic of two traditions—conservative Protestant and historically black churches.

What Else Matters?

Congregations with a healthy heart (i.e., many worshipers feel a strong sense of belonging) have a younger age profile.[6] This is the first strength measure we found related to the age profile of the congregation. Congregations with an older age profile are more likely to have lower scores on the Having a Sense of Belonging Index. This finding suggests younger worshipers are attracted to places that feel like "home" and

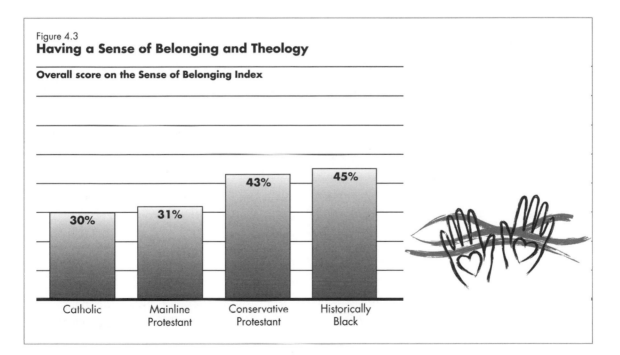

Figure 4.3
Having a Sense of Belonging and Theology

Overall score on the Sense of Belonging Index

Catholic	Mainline Protestant	Conservative Protestant	Historically Black
30%	31%	43%	45%

MYTH TRAP #4

Congregations with older worshipers can count on them to be emotionally attached to their congregation. Congregations with younger worshipers have to work harder to encourage a sense of belonging to the congregation.

Congregations with younger-than-average worshipers score higher on our measure of feeling a sense of belonging. Finding a safe, welcoming "home" in which to worship is a more common experience for younger worshipers. Having a sense of belonging plays a key role in keeping younger worshipers committed and involved.

where friendships are made. Congregations with a younger age profile consist of worshipers whose participation is increasing and whose sense of belonging is growing.

Will Having a Sense of Belonging Help Us Grow in Numbers?

The strength of Having a Sense of Belonging does *not* directly explain numerical growth.[7] As we explored how each strength, independent from other strengths, predicted growing in numbers, the subjective feelings of belonging were less important than some other strengths. Some strengths are more central and directly related to numerical growth. For example, congregations that care deeply for children and youth draw new people like a powerful magnet, so much so that this quality overpowers factors that are more like casting a net to draw new people in more closely. The Having a Sense of Belonging strength is more the latter—important but more subtle in its relationship to numerical growth. Having a Sense of Belonging is likely to play a more important role in retaining the people who are already attending.

Why Having a Sense of Belonging Matters

Congregations with a healthy heart touch the feelings of their participants. Someone said that home, in one of its many forms, is the great object of life. "Home is the place where

WHAT MATTERS FOR BELONGING?		WHO EXCELS?
Congregational size .... Yes	→	Small congregations
Theology .... Yes	→	Conservative Protestant and historically black denomination churches
Age profile of worshipers....... Yes	→	Younger than average
Not related to numerical growth		

we rest; home is the place where we find ourselves; home is the place where we feel safe."[8] Many worshipers find their "home" in their congregation—a place of safety, a place with supportive friends, and a place of acceptance. Strong congregations embrace many people by welcoming them home.

©hris Morgan 2002 cxmedia.com

I SEND MY KIDS
TO CHURCH BECAUSE
I WANT THEM TO
GROW UP RIGHT

I DON'T GO BECAUSE
I FIND IT REPRESSIVE,
JUDGMENTAL AND
SELF-RIGHTEOUS

CHAPTER 5

STRENGTH 5:
CARING FOR CHILDREN AND YOUTH

One generation plants the trees; another gets the shade.

CHINESE PROVERB

Educating young people about faith and the expectations of the faithful is one of the universal purposes of congregations. Faith development does not occur in a vacuum, but rather is cultivated intentionally by a community of faith-filled people. Almost all congregations take specific steps to ensure their children and young people are nurtured by the faith community. Caring for children and youth plays a key role in the ways congregations increase the chances that their youth will remain a part of a faith community as they grow up.

The Caring for Children and Youth Index

The Caring for Children and Youth Index focuses on how a congregation nurtures its young people. Three factors go into this index (see Figure 5.1). Of the three, the largest

Figure 5.1
Caring for Children and Youth

Percentage of Worshipers . . .

Whose children and youth (living at home) also worship here

77%

Who are satisfied with what is offered by the congregation for children and youth (under age 19)

58%

Who report ministry for children or youth as one of the three most valued aspects of their congregation

16%

Overall score on the Caring for Children and Youth Index

50%

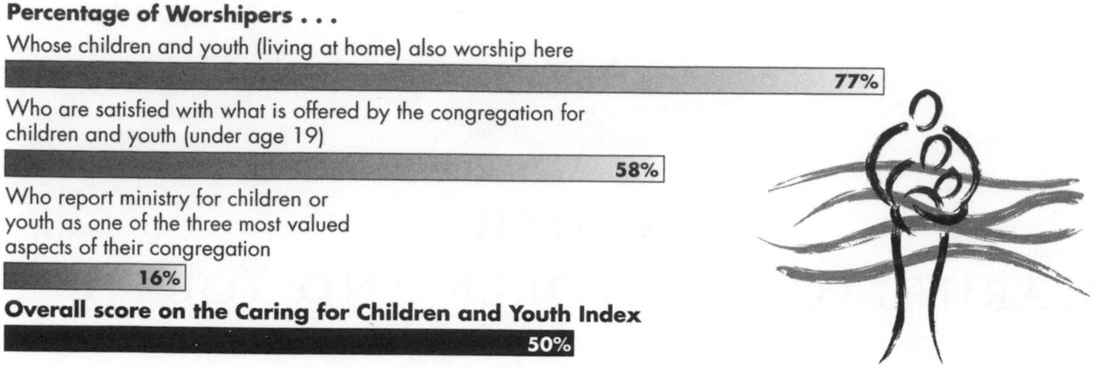

percentage of congregations can celebrate the first factor—retention of children and youth. The percentage of worshipers' children (living at home) who worship in the same congregation reflects the congregation's ability to sustain the participation of their attendees' children and youth. If a congregation cannot involve and retain even its young people, it will probably not do a good job of attracting and retaining adults over the long term. Our findings show that in the average congregation, 77% of worshipers' children also attend there. The remaining 23% may be attending elsewhere or not attending at all.

The second factor in the Caring for Children and Youth Index taps worshipers' satisfaction with what the congregation is offering for children and youth. In the typical congregation, 58% of worshipers report they are satisfied with the congregation's youth programs and activities.

The final factor in the index reflects the percentage of worshipers who say the congregation's ministry for children and youth is one of the three most valued aspects of the congregation. On average, 16% of worshipers chose children and youth ministry as one of their top three values.

As with other indices, this measure of congregational strength is created as an average of the factors that comprise the index. The typical congregation scored 50% on the Caring for Children and Youth Index. Scores can range from 0% to 100%, but most congregations fall between 38% and 63%.

Do congregations do an equally good job of nurturing the next generation of attendees? Yes—most congregations invest in the care of children and youth at similar levels.[1] Some may argue that the quality and quantity of that investment should be much higher. The following sections explore what factors influence congregations to devote their energy toward the future by caring for their young people.

Beyond-the-Ordinary Congregations

What predicts excellence in caring for the next generation?[2] Congregations that score in the top 20% of all congregations on the Caring for Children and Youth Index also have high scores on two other strength indices:

1. Growing spiritually (Strength 1)

2. Sharing a common vision for the congregation's future (Strength 10)

This makes it clear that congregations with their eyes on the future invest in their young attendees and emphasize faith development. In

MYTH TRAP #5

Most congregations view children and youth ministry as very important.

Fewer than one in five worshipers in the typical congregation rate children and youth programs as what they value most about their congregation. If a program, activity, or objective is not a top priority, how much time and resources will a congregation invest in it? Probably not as much as is required. Some congregations have given up on this objective. Yet growing congregations involve children and youth, nurture them in the present, and make a difference in their lives for the future. A very good investment.

the song "The Greatest Love of All," made famous by Whitney Houston, adults are urged to teach the children well, for they are the future.[3] Knowing that Linda Creed, the young mother who penned those lines, was struggling with breast cancer and died before the song hit the charts makes the lyrics particularly poignant. She recognized the important link between caring for young people and focusing on a positive future that we found in strong congregations across the country.

Does Congregational Size Matter?

Does caring for children and youth require a village, as the African proverb says? Do village-size congregations score higher on this index than small, family-size ones? Our results show that on average, mid-size and large congregations excel in caring for their youth, and that small congregations have room to improve on this index. The village

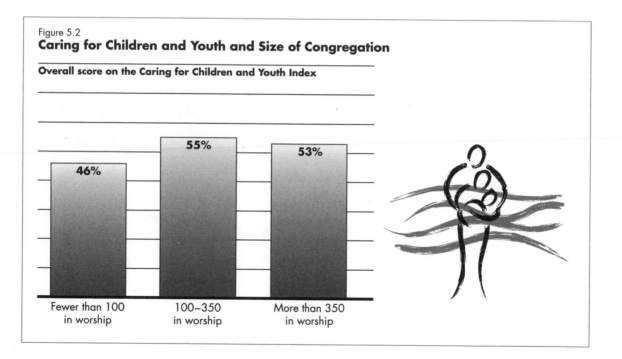

Figure 5.2
Caring for Children and Youth and Size of Congregation

Overall score on the Caring for Children and Youth Index

Fewer than 100 in worship	100–350 in worship	More than 350 in worship
46%	55%	53%

most able to care for a congregation's youth gathers more than 100 in worship (see Figure 5.2). Smaller congregations typically have fewer children and youth, and may have difficulty effectively meeting the needs of a smaller number of children spread across many ages.

Does this difference hold true for the individual factors in the Caring for Children and Youth Index? On each of the specific factors, comparing congregations by size reveals that small congregations tend to score lowest. Worshipers in small congregations are least satisfied with the programs for children and youth. They are least likely to list children's ministry as one of the three most valued aspects of their congregation. A smaller percentage of their children also attend the congregation. Mid-size congregations (with 100 to 350 in worship) score highest on two of the three factors—retention of youth and valuing the congregation's ministry for children. On the third factor—satisfaction with the congregation's programs for children and youth—large and mid-size congregations both exceed the scores of small congregations. Larger congregations, and particularly mid-size congregations, evidence greater strength in their ability to nurture and care for the future generation of worshipers.

Does Congregational Theology Matter?

Do congregations of different faith traditions vary in their scores on the Caring for Children and Youth Index? We found differences across denominational groups on the overall index, as well as on the three specific factors that comprise this strength. On the overall index, conservative Protestant and historically black churches scored highest, mainline Protestant churches were in the middle, and Catholic parishes scored lowest (see Figure 5.3).

A mix of patterns emerged on the three factors in this index. Worshipers in Catholic parishes are less likely than those in conservative Protestant and historically black congregations to report satisfaction with what their congregation offers for children and youth. Mainline Protestant congregations fall in the middle. Fewer worshipers in Catholic parishes than in mainline Protestant, conservative Protestant, or historically

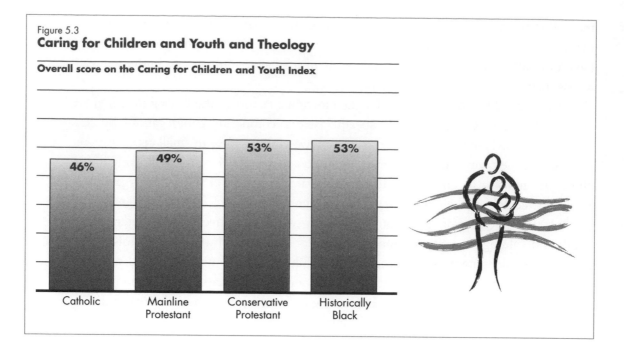

Figure 5.3
Caring for Children and Youth and Theology

Overall score on the Caring for Children and Youth Index

Catholic	Mainline Protestant	Conservative Protestant	Historically Black
46%	49%	53%	53%

black churches list ministry for children and youth as one of the three most valued aspects of the congregation. And finally, Catholic parishes and mainline Protestant churches do not meet the high levels of retention of children and youth exhibited in conservative Protestant and historically black churches.

We anticipated that Catholic parishes would score higher than other groups on the Caring for Children and Youth Index. More than 90% of the Catholic parishes in our study offer religious education classes for children and youth. Nurturing children and youth in the faith of their parents is a deeply held value for Catholics. However, Catholic expectations in this area may be higher—many long for the days when there was a parochial school in nearly every parish. They fondly remember the dedicated women who taught in Catholic schools, and too often feel that the one-hour-per-week parish religious education led by volunteer lay catechists is not enough. Catholics come out low on this index—not because they don't value caring for children and youth, but precisely because they do value so highly religious education for children. They register their dissatisfaction with current parish religious education programs for children and youth and are less likely to list current ministry for children and youth as one of the three most valued aspects of their congregation.[4]

What Else Matters?

Younger congregations, where the average worshiper's age is below the average age of worshipers in all congregations, place greater emphasis on caring for their young people than older congregations, where the typical worshiper's age is above the national average for all worshipers.[5] Younger congregations score higher on the Caring for Children and Youth Index and on the three factors that comprise the index. Younger congregations tend to have a higher percentage of children. This fact encourages the congregation to focus on young people's needs. One of these measures—the percentage of children living at home who also attend the congregation—gives all congregations, regardless of size, an opportunity to care for those in their midst. In the average congregation with a younger age profile, a larger percentage of their children also attend.

Will Caring for Children and Youth Help Us Grow in Numbers?

The answer is a big yes! One of the most powerful predictors of numerical growth in American congregations is their caring for young attendees.[6] Congregations where adults bring their children to services and activities, value ministry with this age group, and believe the current programs are good are more likely to be growing in numbers. Congregations that give the center of their attention to their children and youth can grow in two ways. First, they grow internally—by increasing their chances of retaining some young attendees as they become adults. Second, they grow externally—attracting parents in the community who are looking for high-quality religious education and other activities for their children.

WHAT MATTERS FOR CARING FOR CHILDREN AND YOUTH?	WHO EXCELS?
Congregational size . . . . Yes →	Mid-size congregations
Theology . . . . Yes →	Conservative Protestant and historically black denomination churches
Age profile of worshipers . . . . Yes →	Younger than average

Positive predictor of numerical growth

Why Caring for Children and Youth Matters

A New York subway ad targeted at young people reads: "Want to feed your soul? We've got a great menu." An example of a church's proactive effort targeted at youth, the sign signals the urgency felt by many congregations to find and include younger worshipers. While a significant number of Americans don't regularly attend worship services, young adults are especially likely to be missing.[7] If children and youth are not attending or don't find something to draw them back, the age gap between worshipers and those who don't attend is likely to widen. But there is good news: the majority of today's adolescents have a positive regard for religious activities and the small minority that are hostile to organized religion has not grown in recent decades.[8]

Caring for children and youth also has an immediate benefit. Parents remain committed when a congregation cares for their children. Congregational shoppers face a buyer's market with an expanding range of choices for children's activities. Parents may not remain if their children's needs are not being met, seeking instead to find a congregation that will meet those needs.

Building the faith of children and youth also builds the future congregation. While nurturing young people engages a congregation's heart and provides a focus on the future, many congregations cannot claim it as a strength. The importance of a congregation's children for the congregation's future appears obvious. As children and teenagers become young adults they will take on ever more important roles in the congregation. And the foundation children receive steadies them as they begin their own lives, perhaps in distant locations and new congregations. High mobility rates force congregations to think about ways to create "transportable" commitments to faith communities. By caring for youth, congregations can plant seeds and nourish the seeds of faith that will become tall trees providing shelter for future faith communities.

©hris Morgan   1999   cxmedia.com

CHAPTER 6

STRENGTH 6:
FOCUSING ON THE COMMUNITY

God is doing a new thing, and the church is often the last place people find
out about it.[1]

KENNETH BYERLY

Critics charge that worshiping communities are commonly disconnected from their local
communities. Every congregation exists in a precise place and space. In that way, they are
like no other community of faith in the present, past, or future. How do congregations focus
on the community around them? How do they tend to the "garden outside their doors"?

The Garden outside Our Doors

In what ways do worshipers engage with their neighbors or work to make a difference
in their lives? We asked worshipers about ways they work in their neighborhood
"garden." Many worshipers (26% in the average congregation) organize through their
congregation to provide diverse types of community service. For example, they may
serve meals in a soup kitchen, give away warm clothes, or take part in advocacy groups

Conservative Protestant congregations focus mostly on their surrounding community— by caring for those in need and by inviting people to attend worship services.

Theology makes a difference in the type of lens congregations use when they focus on their local community. Mainline Protestant and historically black denomination churches engage with their communities by caring for others and advocating on behalf of those in need. Conservative Protestants typically use a different type of lens. Their community focal point involves worshipers talking about their faith and inviting people to participate in church activities. Some congregations turn inward, concerning themselves with what happens inside their doors. But strong congregations use a wide-angle lens to balance their attention between the ministries inside their walls and their ministry in the world.

(e.g., promoting better public education for children). Surprisingly, we found a higher percentage of worshipers in the average congregation (28%) working with social service or advocacy groups *not* associated with the congregation. In addition to serving their communities through groups, people work in informal ways with their neighbors to solve problems related to safety, access to government services, or similar issues. A slightly smaller percentage of worshipers (21%) in the average congregation are engaged with their neighborhood in this way—on their own, not as part of a group.

Worshipers also vote. Voting represents another way people in congregations provide nutrients to enrich their community's soil. In fact, worshipers are more likely to vote than the average American.[2] While only half of all Americans voted in the 2000 presidential election, three out of four worshipers made it to the polls. Giving to charitable causes is another individual act that makes a difference in a community. Most worshipers—two out of three in the average congregation—give money to community groups and causes (in addition to their contributions to the congregation).

Values determine which strengths a congregation builds and maintains. But long-held and deeply rooted values can be so powerful they also prevent positive change from happening. Values "show where your boundaries are; they translate into standards of behavior and expectations."[3] In some instances, an internal focus keeps the congregation from looking outward toward the community. On the other hand, placing a high value on being community-focused may continue even when the environment changes. In such cases, the changing needs of the community may require new strategies to effectively meet those needs.

Two final questions reflect the value worshipers place on being involved and integrated with the local community. Only one in ten people checked ministry to the community as something they most value about their congregation. But this is a middle-of-the-road ranking compared to the list of values we provided in the survey. The second community-focused value—openness to social diversity—reflects a desire to be open to others whether or not they are like existing members. Compared to others we asked about, this value ranks at the lower end.[4]

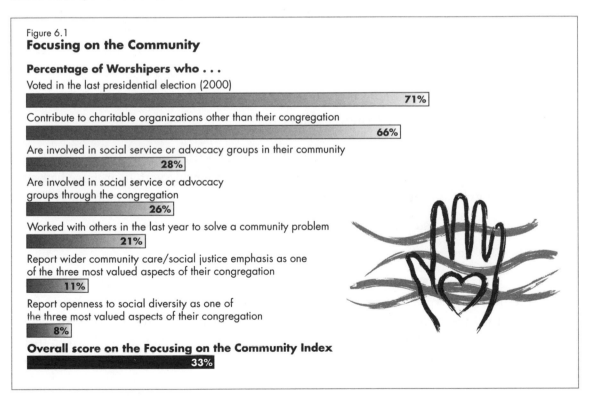

Figure 6.1
Focusing on the Community

Percentage of Worshipers who . . .
Voted in the last presidential election (2000)
71%

Contribute to charitable organizations other than their congregation
66%

Are involved in social service or advocacy groups in their community
28%

Are involved in social service or advocacy
groups through the congregation
26%

Worked with others in the last year to solve a community problem
21%

Report wider community care/social justice emphasis as one
of the three most valued aspects of their congregation
11%

Report openness to social diversity as one of
the three most valued aspects of their congregation
8%

Overall score on the Focusing on the Community Index
33%

The Focusing on the Community Index

How can we describe the breadth and depth of a congregation's focus on the community? The seven facets described above form the congregation's community lens—the Focusing on the Community Index. The typical congregation has a score of 33% on this index (see Figure 6.1). This average score takes on significance when we examine how it might change among congregations of different size or theology, or when other features of the congregation vary.

Do most congregations engage with their communities at the same level? Yes, scores on this index are fairly similar. The range of how much congregations are focusing on the community is not large. Most congregations fall within about 9 percentage points on either side of the average score of 33%.[5] When we ranked the ten congregational strengths in order from how congregations are most alike to how they are least alike, the Focusing on the Community Index is the third from the top, which shows congregations are relatively alike on this measure. Congregations are more similar only in the areas of meaningful worship (Strength 2) and participating in the congregation (Strength 3).

Beyond-the-Ordinary Congregations

Congregations and parishes in the top 20% on the Focusing on the Community Index are beyond the ordinary or above-average in their relationship with their immediate surroundings.[6] Congregations in this top 20% have worshipers who are more likely to:

1. Have a strong sense of belonging to the congregation (Strength 4)

2. Have empowering congregational leaders (Strength 9)

This mix of strengths connotes that these congregations have successfully answered the question, "What is unique about this congregation?" Leaders and worshipers have discerned their congregational mission for their location. "Franchising," or borrowing a successful approach used elsewhere, seems faster and easier. After all, if it worked there, it should work here.[7] But leaders in strong congregations recognize the irreplaceable assets and resources in their local community. And as empowering leaders, they help attendees recognize their own one-of-a-kind talents that make them potential partners for working in their community. The match between the assets and needs of the community and the contributions of the congregation cannot be duplicated.

Does Congregational Size Matter?

Does the size of the congregation have anything to do with the strength of the congregation's focus on the community? Do larger congregations till more soil? The answer is no. A typical small congregation (fewer than 100 in worship) is not very different from a large congregation (more than 350 in worship) in the extent to which they focus on the community. But differences do emerge on some of the specific factors that comprise the Focusing on the Community Index. Surprisingly, mid-size congregations on average have larger percentages of people participating in social service groups, voting, giving to charitable causes, and expressing values supportive of a strong community focus than small congregations. What makes mid-size congregations turn to face their communities and see them more clearly? Perhaps the size is just right for maximizing the balance between a large enough pool of volunteers to draw on and a small enough community to discourage "free riders," members who enjoy the benefits of the faith community with little or no investment.

Does Congregational Theology Matter?

The ways in which congregations interact with their communities emerge from their theological views about their fundamental mission. For example, mainline Protestant congregations typically score the highest on the Focusing on the Community Index (see Figure 6.2). Their emphasis on the social mandate of the gospel tends to be stronger than their emphasis on evangelizing others. Historically black churches score slightly lower, but the differences between these two theological families are not significant. The average conservative Protestant congregation has the lowest score on the index. While conservative

Protestant congregations' scores on the previous strength measures (see chapters 1 to 5) have been the highest, focusing on the community is generally not one of their strengths.

Yet no congregation can afford to ignore its context or those in the surrounding community. Theologically, "selfishness is alien to the nature" and mission of a congregation. Congregations that live only for themselves are "starting a trip toward extinction. . . . They will eventually die of spiritual asphyxiation because they lack the oxygen of love."[8]

What Else Matters?

The age profile of congregations influences how congregations act on their faith. Younger congregations (i.e., average age at or below the national median of fifty-two for all congregational attendees) are actually *less* likely to be focusing on their communities than older congregations (i.e., average age above the national median).[9] Perhaps younger congrega-

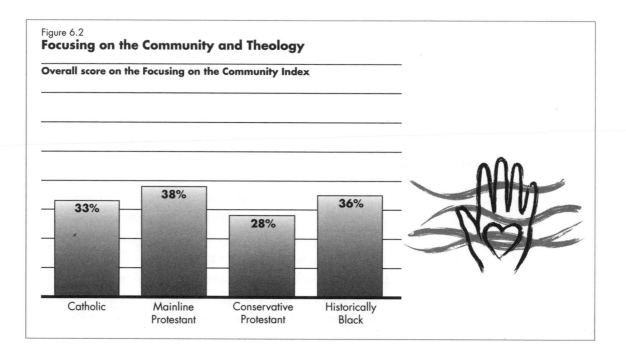

Figure 6.2
Focusing on the Community and Theology

Overall score on the Focusing on the Community Index

Catholic: 33%
Mainline Protestant: 38%
Conservative Protestant: 28%
Historically Black: 36%

┌───┐

WHAT MATTERS FOR FOCUSING ON THE COMMUNITY?

WHO EXCELS?

Congregational size . . . . No

Theology . . . . Yes → Mainline Protestant churches

Age profile of worshipers . . . . Yes → Older than average

Negative predictor of numerical growth

└───┘

tions have more internal needs (e.g., more children's programming) and fewer resources (i.e., younger worshipers have less discretionary income and often less time). But younger congregations are likely to be more similar to their surrounding community, especially in age, and thus have to work less hard on maintaining a relationship with their neighbors.[10]

Does Focusing on the Community Help Us Grow in Numbers?

Congregations sometimes feel tension between taking care of present members and seeking or serving new people outside their doors. Unfortunately, we found congregations that focused on the community were *less* likely to be growing in numbers.[11] Why would this be the case? Congregations focusing on the community were also less likely to be strong in other areas related to growth—caring for children and youth and welcoming new people. But just because this currently tends to be the case does not mean the strength of focusing on the community should be left out of the mix of ingredients congregations combine for their location and mission. All ten strengths are just that—real strengths of American congregations. And these strengths do not appear alone in the real world of congregational life. This complexity reflects the current realities of how congregations balance the change and diversity that challenge them.

Why Focusing on the Community Matters

Congregations focusing on their communities experience long, fruitful seasons of sowing and harvesting. Like expert gardeners, congregations know what strategies produce a thriving garden in their climate and location. Uniquely embedded in a community context, beyond-the-ordinary congregations thrive with and through their local gardens. Strong congregations reflect George Bernard Shaw's words: "[M]y life belongs to the community, and as long as I live it is my privilege to do for it whatever I can."[12] Strong congregations are "down to earth," doing all that is possible to improve the present and future lives of those in their communities.

©hris Morgan 2003

cxmedia.com

CHAPTER 7

STRENGTH 7:
SHARING FAITH

Each of us has an enormous need to connect with God yet we rarely consider this possibility without assistance. More often, someone puts up a signpost pointing us in that direction.[1]

HERB MILLER

How important is it for a congregation to seek out new people to join their community of faith? All organizations, including religious congregations, need a flow of new people to ensure continued existence. Yet congregations do not place equal emphasis on reaching out and recruiting others. "Evangelism," "reaching the unchurched," "witnessing," and "sharing the good news" are some of the expressions used to describe an intentional approach for sharing faith, attracting others, and welcoming new people. Many congregations use advertising and other media-based methods of outreach. But most new worshipers report that a personal invitation to worship is what brought them through the doors the very first time. How do worshipers share their hearts and their faith with others?

The Sharing Faith Index

The Sharing Faith Index reflects a congregation's strength in reaching out to people who might potentially become part of their faith community. Our analyses identified four factors that go into this index (see Figure 7.1). The results of these factors include:

- A majority of worshipers in the typical congregation (60%) report that in the previous year they invited to a worship service someone who doesn't currently attend worship anywhere.

- About one-quarter of worshipers in the average congregation feel comfortable talking about their faith and seek opportunities to do so. (Another half of worshipers feel comfortable talking about their faith, but do so only if it comes up in conversation. This percentage of worshipers was not included in the calculation of the overall index score.)

- Similarly, about one in five say they're involved in their congregation's outreach or evangelism activities.

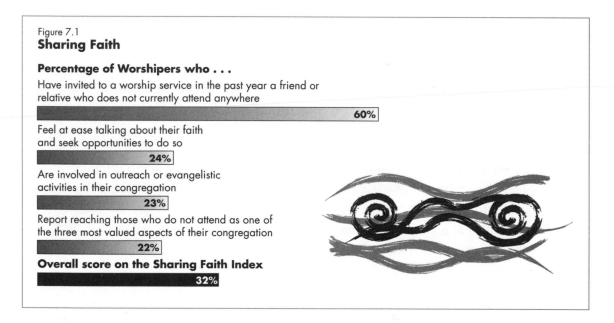

Figure 7.1
Sharing Faith

Percentage of Worshipers who . . .

Have invited to a worship service in the past year a friend or relative who does not currently attend anywhere
60%

Feel at ease talking about their faith and seek opportunities to do so
24%

Are involved in outreach or evangelistic activities in their congregation
23%

Report reaching those who do not attend as one of the three most valued aspects of their congregation
22%

Overall score on the Sharing Faith Index
32%

■ And finally, one in four rate their congregation's efforts to reach those who don't attend as one of the three most valued aspects of the congregation.

When these four factors are combined, the average congregation scores 32% on the Sharing Faith Index. Congregations can score potentially between 0% and 100%, but in actuality the highest score among participating congregations was just 67%. There is a fair amount of diversity on this index across congregations. Most fall within 15 percentage points of the average of 32%.[2] Only one index shows greater variability among congregations: the Welcoming New People Index (see chapter 8). Congregations display remarkable differences in the extent to which they can claim this strength. Clearly, many factors determine why congregations value sharing faith with others and how they act on this value.

Beyond-the-Ordinary Congregations

MYTH TRAP #7

Congregations grow because the majority of their worshipers are inviting others to attend worship services.

Congregations grow numerically for many reasons. For example, quality programs for children and youth and meaningful worship services draw new people like powerful magnets. But how do people find out what a congregation has to offer? Most people visit a congregation for the first time because someone they know invited them. However, these visitors need a reason to return a second and third time. A congregation grows because something of value is offered to newcomers.

What other strengths do congregations in the top 20% of congregations on the Sharing Faith Index also possess?[3] Such congregations are more likely to have worshipers who:

1. Participate in congregational activities (Strength 3)

2. Have a strong sense of belonging to the congregation (Strength 4)

3. Have empowering congregational leaders (Strength 9)

4. Have begun attending the congregation in the last five years (Strength 8)

This constellation of related strengths reveals a complex pattern of behaviors and experiences. For instance, congregations where worshipers are comfortable talking about their faith have more newcomers than other congregations. Is this because faith sharing and outreach have been effective in welcoming new people? Probably so. But the reverse may also be true: New people, because of the enthusiasm they bring, may encourage all worshipers to talk about the positives they are experiencing there—including their spiritual growth. Those personal conversations help build relationships among worshipers that foster their sense of belonging. And empowering leaders share the message that all who participate in a congregation are responsible for reaching out to others.

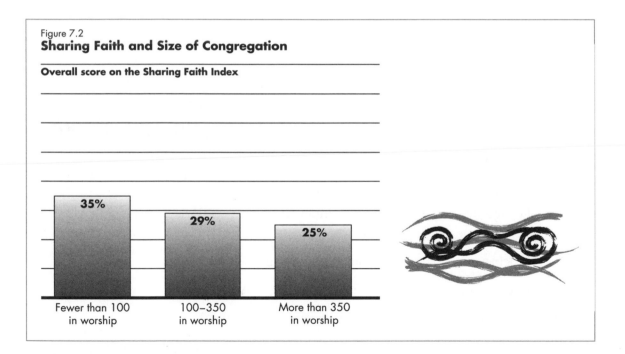

Figure 7.2
Sharing Faith and Size of Congregation

Overall score on the Sharing Faith Index

35% — Fewer than 100 in worship
29% — 100–350 in worship
25% — More than 350 in worship

Does Congregational Size Matter?

What impact does congregational size have on Sharing Faith? Scores on this index are higher among small congregations (with fewer than 100 in worship) than among mid-size and large congregations (see Figure 7.2). The same pattern emerged on three of the four factors in this scale: having invited someone to worship in the last year, seeking opportunities to talk about faith, and valuing the congregation's outreach ministries. For the exception—involvement in congregational evangelism activities—both small and mid-size and congregations scored higher than large ones.

These findings imply that in smaller congregations individual worshipers feel they carry more of the burden for congregational outreach. In a small congregation there are fewer people to share the load. If the congregation is to succeed in bringing in new worshipers, everyone must take on faith sharing as part of their personal mission.

Does Congregational Theology Matter?

Common perception holds that conservative Protestant churches excel at taking their message to the unchurched. Is this a myth we can shatter? Actually, this belief is true. Large differences emerged across faith groups on the Sharing Faith Index and its composite factors. Conservative Protestant churches do in fact outpace their congregational siblings in this area, with the exception of historically black congregations (see Figure 7.3). On the overall Sharing Faith Index, conservative Protestant and historically black churches score 20 percentage points higher than either Catholic parishes or mainline churches.

This pattern repeats itself on the individual items in the scale. On each one, conservative Protestant and historically black churches score on average 15 to 25 percentage points higher than the next highest faith group. Worshipers in these congregations are more likely than those elsewhere to invite others to worship, talk about their faith, take part in evangelism activities of their congregation, and say their congregation's efforts to reach those outside their doors are one of the three most valued aspects of the congregation.

The differences between Catholic parishes and mainline Protestant churches, though much smaller, are nonetheless statistically significant for three of the four factors. More worshipers in Catholic parishes than in mainline Protestant churches feel comfortable talking about their faith and seek opportunities to do so. More worshipers in mainline churches than in Catholic parishes participate in congregational evangelism activities and invite others to worship.

Congregations of all faith groups have before them an opportunity to learn something about what makes conservative Protestant and historically black congregations so strong in this area. Some congregations may find certain faith-sharing practices of conservative Protestant churches to be beyond their comfort zone. Yet, with an open mind

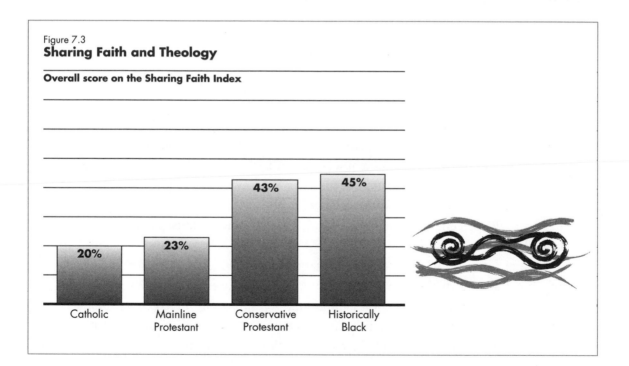

Figure 7.3
Sharing Faith and Theology

Overall score on the Sharing Faith Index

- Catholic: 20%
- Mainline Protestant: 23%
- Conservative Protestant: 43%
- Historically Black: 45%

and creativity, most congregations can find something of value in the habits of strong faith-sharing congregations.

What Else Matters?

Are older worshipers more likely to talk with others about their faith? Or are younger worshipers more likely to invite their friends and family to worship services? The age profile of the congregation is irrelevant to scores on the Sharing Faith Index. Older congregations (where the average age is above fifty-two) are just as likely as younger congregations to share their faith, be concerned with those not currently attending, and invite them to come to worship services.[4]

Will Sharing Faith Help Us Grow in Numbers?

This question is really two questions: What gets people to visit a congregation for the first time? And what causes a congregation to grow numerically? Almost everyone attends a congregation for the first time because someone they know—a family member, friend, neighbor, or coworker—invited them. Conservative Protestants share their faith and invite others to worship with greater frequency than worshipers in other faith groups. Does their behavior explain why conservative Protestant churches grow faster than congregations in other denominations? Probably not. According to this survey, conservative Protestant churches are more likely to have some of the powerful magnets that attract and retain new worshipers—quality programs for children and youth and meaningful worship. Thus, once conservative Protestants invite a friend or family member to their congregation, their visitors have the kind of positive experiences that make them want to return again and again.

When the impact of all ten strengths on numerical growth is considered, sharing faith becomes a negative predictor of growing in numbers.[5] What explains this finding? Inviting others to worship is only half of the equation of what makes a congregation

WHAT MATTERS FOR SHARING FAITH?		WHO EXCELS?
Congregational size . . . . Yes	→	Small congregations
Theology . . . . Yes	→	Conservative Protestant and historically black denomination churches
Age profile of worshipers . . . . . . No		

Negative predictor of numerical growth

grow. Once people visit, they must find something of value if they are going to return for a second time and beyond. Like the old sales adage, "you can only sell a dead horse once," inviting someone to a lifeless congregation makes only one sale—one visit—and almost guarantees no "repeat customers."

Explaining congregational growth is not straightforward. Congregational life is a complex system in which everything is related. When you take into account how much Sharing Faith explains growth, other strengths are more central and relate more directly to numerical growth. Some strengths are powerhouse strengths (e.g., Caring for Children and Youth) that dwarf the potential influence of the individual worshiper actions as measured by the Sharing Faith Index.

Why Sharing Faith Matters

Worshipers are called to grow in their faith—"by relearning and reinforcing what they already understand faith to be and by expanding, deepening, and even correcting initial understandings of faith."[6] Faith grows through time spent in worship and reflection, by responding to difficult life circumstances, and through talking with others about the meaning of faith. We found only one in four worshipers feel at ease talking about their faith and seek opportunities to do so. What about other worshipers? About half of all worshipers feel mostly at ease talking about their faith, but only do so if it comes up in coversation.

Yet sharing faith is not easy. When meeting new people we often describe ourselves in terms of what we do—the roles we fill at work and in our families and the activities we pursue in our leisure time. It's harder to talk about our values and our faith. Many of us feel that living our faith is enough—that if we honor God in our daily activities, we need not be involved in personal faith sharing. Yet, without a personal invitation, few new people walk through a congregation's doors for the first time. And without sharing how our faith shapes our everyday lives, we miss the opportunity to "map the trail" for others.

REVERSE EVANGELISM WAS DISCOVERED BY REV DRAKE.
A STUDY OF NIGHTCLUBS SHOWED THAT TO ATTRACT YOUNG PEOPLE,
THE CHURCH HAD TO BE VERY DIFFICULT TO GET IN TO.

©hris Morgan 2002 cxmedia.com

CHAPTER 8

STRENGTH 8:
WELCOMING NEW PEOPLE

An innovative congregation nurtures new ways of looking at new things, new ways of looking at old things, and old ways of looking at new things. It is constantly looking for new lay leadership who can bring new perspectives from the edges of the congregation.[1]

GEORGE BULLARD

How do people become wealthy? By earning more than they spend. That simple answer to a complex question holds a grain of truth. How do congregations grow? By bringing in more new people than they lose. Again, it's a simplified look at a complex issue. Most congregations lose at least a few worshipers each year—some die; others move away for jobs, college, or love; and sometimes people just stop coming. If a congregation is to maintain its current size, it must replace those who leave. If a congregation is to grow, it must bring in more new people than are lost through attrition or death. But new people are more than just numbers. They bring new perspectives, energy, resources, and talent to the congregation. Are congregations also welcoming new people into service and leadership?

The Welcoming New People Index

The eighth strength we identified is the ability of congregations to bring new worshipers into their midst. Unlike the other strengths, just one factor measures this strength—the percentage of worshipers who began attending the congregation in the last five years. In the typical congregation, one-third of worshipers are newcomers. That means that the typical congregation has a score of 33% on the Welcoming New People Index (see Figure 8.1).

But as you can imagine, some congregations are doing better than others at adding new people to their faith community. There is considerable variation on this index. Most congregations fall within 17 percentage points on either side of the average score of 33%—that is, they score between about 16% and 51%. Imagine the difference between a congregation where 16% of worshipers are new in the last five years and a church where half of worshipers started attending in that time period![2]

What do we know about new people? Those who began attending in the last five years tend to be younger and more educated than other worshipers; they are less likely to be married and more likely to be working full- or part-time; and they typically have lower levels of participation and involvement in the congregation. But they look just like other worshipers in terms of gender, income, race and ethnicity, and place of birth.[3]

Figure 8.1
Welcoming New People

Overall score on the Welcoming New People Index
33%

New people fall into four categories: first-timers, returnees, switchers, and transfers. In the typical congregation, about 9% of worshipers who started attending there in the last five years can be described as first-timers—those with no faith background whatsoever. About 23% are returnees—those who attended at some time in the past, but just prior to coming to their current congregation were not attending anywhere. Another 30% are switchers—those who have changed denominations or faith groups in coming to their current congregation (from Baptist to Methodist or from Catholic to Episcopal, for example). And finally, 39% are transfers—those who changed from one congregation to another within the same denomination or faith group (from First Presbyterian Church in Atlanta to Westminster Presbyterian Church in Tacoma, for example). The profile of new people in a congregation has significant implications. What would a new member class look like if most of a congregation's new people were transfers? Think of the larger challenge if most were switchers or first-timers.

Beyond-the-Ordinary Congregations

Welcoming New People is strongly related to three other strengths.[4] Congregations that score in the top 20% on this strength are more likely to have worshipers who:

1. Invite others to worship and feel at ease talking about their faith (Strength 7)

2. Have a strong vision for the congregation's future (Strength 10)

3. Care for children and youth (Strength 5)

Inviting others is an important first step toward increasing the number of new people. And there may be a reverse relationship as well—new people may be the best at sharing their faith and inviting others to experience what they've found in their new faith community. Strong congregations offer a compelling vision for the future that captures the imagination of new people. Caring for children and youth attracts parents who desire quality programming for their family. And congregations that care for children and youth plant seeds for the next generation of congregational leaders.

Does Congregational Size Matter?

Do the rich get richer? Do large congregations do a better job of attracting new people? Is everyone flocking to the mega-churches across the country? Actually, no. Although the *total number* of new people who attend large congregations is greater than in mid-size and small congregations, the percentage of new people is unrelated to congregational size. That means that large and small congregations have about the same percentage of new worshipers in their pews.

But congregations of different sizes attract different types of new people. The percentage of new people who are first-timers and returnees is not related to congregational size, but the percentage of switchers and transfers is. Smaller congregations attract more switchers than do mid-size and large congregations. And large congregations attract more transfers than do mid-size and small congregations. While congregations of varying sizes are similar in the percentage of new people overall, they differ on the types of new people who attend there.

MYTH TRAP #8

Large congregations attract new people at faster rates than smaller congregations.

In fact, the percentage or proportion of new people in a congregation is unrelated to size. Small and mid-size congregations attract the same share of newcomers as larger congregations. Of course, bigger congregations draw more people in simple numbers, and that increase is more visibly dramatic. In reality, conservative Protestant churches welcome the highest percentage of new people—almost four in ten worshipers are new in the last five years.

Does Congregational Theology Matter?

Many people believe that evangelical congregations have the market cornered on new worshipers. But does theology really play a role in the percentage of new people in a congregation? We found that conservative Protestant congregations do, in fact, have higher than average scores on the Welcoming New People Index, and that historically black congregations have lower scores. As Figure 8.2 shows, almost four in ten

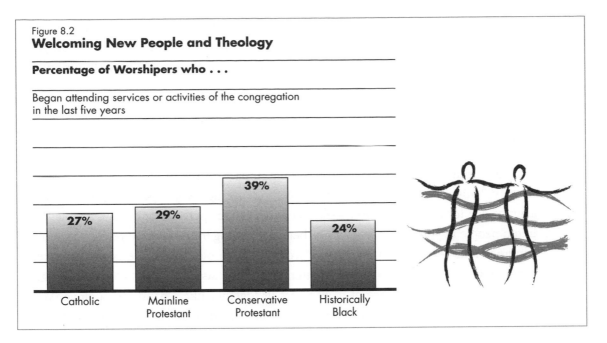

Figure 8.2
Welcoming New People and Theology

Percentage of Worshipers who . . .

Began attending services or activities of the congregation
in the last five years

Catholic	Mainline Protestant	Conservative Protestant	Historically Black
27%	29%	39%	24%

worshipers in conservative Protestant churches are new in the last five years. In historically black congregations, just slightly more than two in ten are new people.

The specific types of new people vary among congregations with different theologies, too. Although historically black churches claim a slightly larger percentage of first-timers, this difference is not statistically significant. Contrary to expectations, no faith tradition is doing an outstanding job of attracting those who have never been part of a faith community. It's a challenge for congregations of all theologies to find ways to identify and welcome people who have never attended anywhere before. How can congregations ensure that their services are inviting and fulfilling to people who are searching for meaning in their lives?

There are significant differences by faith tradition for the three other types of new people. Mainline Protestant churches do the best job of attracting returnees; conservative Protestant and historically black churches surpass the others in attracting switchers; and Catholic parishes draw the largest percentage of transfers. We shouldn't be surprised to find that Catholics parishes bring in larger percentages of transfers. Many have noted that switching among Protestant groups is much more common than crossing the

Protestant/Catholic divide, and our findings support that belief. But why do mainline Protestant churches attract so many returnees? Many left mainline Protestant congregations and are now interested in returning. Some left other types of congregations and are now exploring what a different faith tradition might offer.

What Else Matters?

The age profile of the congregation has a big impact on the numbers of new people in the pew.[5] Younger congregations—those with an average worshiper age at or below the average age for all congregations—have a much higher percentage of new people. Four in ten people in younger congregations began attending in the last five years. But in older congregations—those with an average worshiper age older than the typical congregation—only one in four people began attending in the last five years. The average age of worshipers and the presence of newcomers fit together like a hand and a glove. When worshipers are older, fewer newcomers are found in their midst. When worshipers are younger, many new people share the pews.

Will Welcoming New People Help Us Grow in Numbers?

New people are just half of the equation. The precious balance between earning money and spending money keeps us solvent. The precious balance between new people and departing people keeps congregations stable or helps them grow. Unfortunately, we have no measure of the number of people who left these congregations in the last five years—those going out the door, never to return, remain uncounted.

It's logical to assume that congregations with more new people are growing, but is that the case, or are such congregations losing as many people as they're drawing in? As it turns out, scores on the Welcoming New People Index were powerful predictors of numerical growth. Most congregations with high percentages of newcomers were also growing numerically. That means congregations successful in bringing in new people also tend to welcome enough newcomers to offset any losses.[6]

Congregational size . . . . No

Theology . . . . Yes → Conservative Protestant and historically
black denomination churches

Age profile of worshipers . . . . Yes → Younger than average

Positive predictor of numerical growth

Yet some congregations welcoming many new people also experience huge losses of attendees and members. These losses may be beyond their control—a major industry in the area relocates, taking away people and jobs; continued urbanization draws younger people away from rural areas; the neighborhood has a high mobility rate; or the older age profile of the congregation makes losses through death a significant factor. Such congregations may be doing a good job of attracting new people but simply cannot keep pace with their membership losses.

Why Welcoming New People Matters

While growth may not be what all congregations desire, few if any want to see their numbers dwindle. A congregation cannot maintain its size or grow if no new people are joining the faithful.

What draws new people into a faith community? Experiences that can be found only in congregations. In *The God We Never Knew*, Marcus Borg describes one such experience: "When worship is functioning as it should, it can be a powerful mediator of the sacred. It can open the heart, shape the religious imagination, and nourish the spiritual life, all within the experience of community."[7] Strong and innovative congregations offer community faith experiences that welcome new people and new perspectives.

©hris Morgan   1997

cxmedia.com

CHAPTER 9

STRENGTH 9:
EMPOWERING LEADERSHIP

Leadership is not so much about technique and methods as it is about opening the heart. Leadership is about inspiration—of oneself and of others. . . . [I]t is a human activity that comes from the heart and considers the hearts of others.[1]

LANCE SECRETAN

Managing and leading any organization is always a complex task. But leadership in voluntary organizations like congregations involves working with a combination of paid staff and volunteers. Pastoral leaders—priests, ministers, rabbis, and others—work together with lay leaders to discern where God is calling the congregation and to keep it on track and moving forward. Yet many things can derail a congregation—conflict, resistance to change, difficulty in thinking creatively about the congregation's path, and so forth. Leadership has been defined as "the art of mobilizing others to want to struggle for shared aspirations."[2] And it's the "want to" aspect of the definition that stands out. An autocratic leader compels others to act in certain ways by promises or threats. But to get others to do something because they *want to* is surely a gift. In this chapter we explore the factors that make up effective congregational leadership.

The Empowering Leadership Index

Four factors capture the nature of a congregation's leadership (see Figure 9.1). The factor that the largest percentage of worshipers affirm is that their leader (pastor, priest, rabbi, etc.) takes into account the ideas of worshipers to a great extent. In the average congregation, 54% believe that the leaders take into account worshipers' ideas to a great extent.

Second, almost as many strongly agree that there is a good match between the congregation and the pastor, priest, or rabbi. (In the average congregation, a total of four out of five worshipers agree—strongly agree or agree—that this is a good match.)

Third, one-half of worshipers in a typical congregation describe the style of leadership of their pastor or priest as one that inspires others to take action. Imagine the impact of leaders with other leadership styles. A leader who tends to take charge in an overcontrolling way would dramatically change the nature and feel of a congregation. The empowering role of laity in such congregations would be greatly diminished. And leaders who sit back passively waiting for others to take action defy the definition of leader-

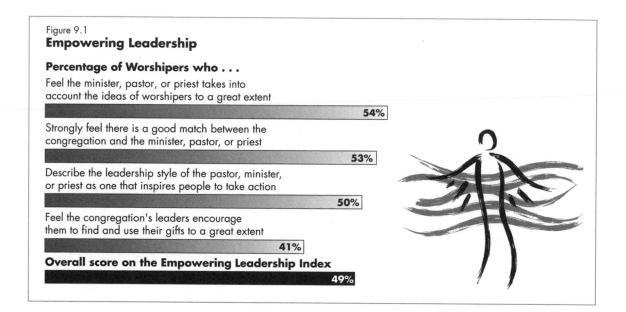

Figure 9.1
Empowering Leadership

Percentage of Worshipers who . . .

Feel the minister, pastor, or priest takes into
account the ideas of worshipers to a great extent
54%

Strongly feel there is a good match between the
congregation and the minister, pastor, or priest
53%

Describe the leadership style of the pastor, minister,
or priest as one that inspires people to take action
50%

Feel the congregation's leaders encourage
them to find and use their gifts to a great extent
41%

Overall score on the Empowering Leadership Index
49%

ship. Inspiring others to action goes far in affirming the critical role of laity in congregational leadership.

Finally, about 41% of worshipers in the average congregation feel the congregation's leaders—whether ordained or lay—encourage them to find and use their gifts for ministry. All worshipers have something to offer their faith communities, whether it's serving as an usher, telephoning shut-ins, organizing the church school program, or making coffee. Freeing worshipers to identify the special way they can make a contribution of time and talent goes far in helping a congregation accomplish its mission.

How do these four factors go together? The overall Empowering Leadership Index averages 49% across congregations. Congregations vary a fair amount on this measure. Most fall within about 16 percentage points of the average score.[3]

MYTH TRAP #9

The most important congregational strength is empowering leadership.

Congregational strengths are interwoven, and each one contributes to extraordinary patterns of excellence. Empowering leadership plays a key role in pushing congregations into the top 20%—the beyond-the-ordinary range. But other strengths are just as essential for promoting effectiveness. For example, Strength 1, Growing Spiritually, predicts congregational dynamics in four other areas of strength! Tending to just one strength guarantees a meager strategy doomed to meager results.

Beyond-the-Ordinary Congregations

What produces excellent congregational leadership? Congregations scoring in the top 20% of all congregations on the Empowering Leadership Index also possess other strengths.[4] In fact, Empowering Leadership is related to several other strengths. Compared to worshipers elsewhere, worshipers in such congregations are more likely to:

1.   Experience meaningful worship (Strength 2)

2. Share a strong vision for the congregation's future (Strength 10)

3. Be involved in the community (Strength 6)

In multiple ways, strong congregations and their leaders—both clergy and laity—work together to ensure the congregation's heart and mind are fully involved.

Does Congregational Size Matter?

What impact does congregational size have on a congregation's Empowering Leadership score? Do worshipers in large congregations, where lots of people may want to "stir the soup," feel less empowered? Our findings show that the smallest congregations (with fewer than 100 in worship) have overall Empowering Leadership scores that are higher than mid-size and large congregations (see Figure 9.2).

Small congregations have higher scores than large and mid-size congregations on

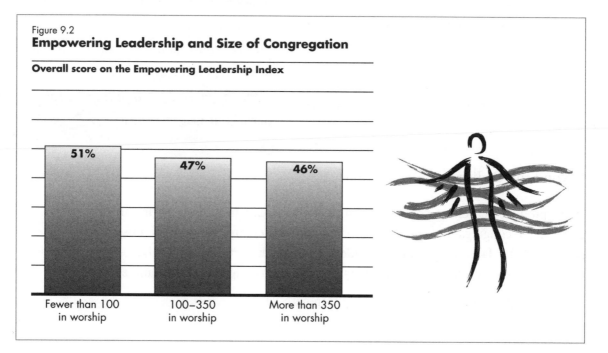

Figure 9.2
Empowering Leadership and Size of Congregation

Overall score on the Empowering Leadership Index

Fewer than 100 in worship	100–350 in worship	More than 350 in worship
51%	47%	46%

two specific factors, too. The sense that leaders encourage worshipers to find and use their gifts in the congregation and the belief that leaders take into account the ideas of others are both higher in small congregations.

This consistent pattern reveals that smaller congregations excel overall and on two of the four factors comprising the Empowering Leadership Index. Small congregations provide a smaller worshiper-to-leader ratio, and this may have a positive impact on worshipers' sense that they play an important role in where the congregation is going. Nonetheless, worshipers in congregations of all sizes are similar in their belief that there is a good match between the congregation and its leader and the sense that the leader inspires others to action.

Does Congregational Theology Matter?

Does faith tradition influence a congregation's Empowering Leadership score? Not surprisingly, it does. Conservative Protestant congregations and historically black congregations score higher than Catholic parishes and mainline Protestant churches on this index (see Figure 9.3). There is little difference between Catholic parishes and mainline Protestant churches, and historically black congregations don't differ significantly from conservative Protestant churches.

Looking at the specific factors in this index reveals a complex pattern of differences and similarities. Significant differences emerged among congregations with different faith traditions on each of the four questions that comprise this index. In general, conservative Protestant congregations score higher than other congregations and Catholic parishes score lower. Mainline Protestant churches tend to fall closer to Catholic parishes than to conservative Protestant churches. The lower scores of Catholic parishes may reflect the impact of assigned (as opposed to called) pastoral leadership. That some mainline Protestant denominations—the United Methodist Church, for example—also assign clergy to congregations may be contributing to the somewhat lower scores among these congregations, as well.

What Else Matters?

Is the style of leadership exercised in a congregation related to the ages of the worshipers? Younger congregations and older congregations are similar in the ways worshipers and leaders engage each other. An empowering leadership style can be found in any congregation, regardless of worshipers' ages. However, worshipers in younger congregations are especially likely to feel their gifts and contributions are welcomed.[5]

Will Empowering Leadership Help Us Grow in Numbers?

We did not find a direct link between empowering leadership and numerical growth in congregations.[6] Does this mean type and style of leadership are unimportant? Absolutely not! Congregational strengths do not exist alone, one by one, in the real world of faith communities. Because of the large number of strengths that predict empowering con-

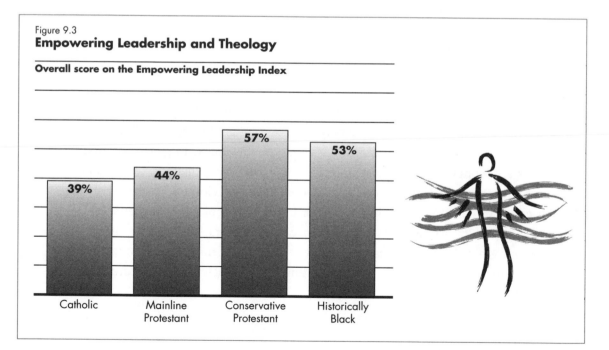

Figure 9.3
Empowering Leadership and Theology

Overall score on the Empowering Leadership Index

- Catholic: 39%
- Mainline Protestant: 44%
- Conservative Protestant: 57%
- Historically Black: 53%

WHAT MATTERS FOR
EMPOWERING LEADERSHIP?   WHO EXCELS?

Congregational size . . . . Yes ➡ Small congregations

Theology . . . . Yes ➡ Conservative Protestant and historically
                                                black denomination churches

Age profile of worshipers . . . . . . No

Not related to numerical growth

gregational leadership, it's clear that the strength of empowering leadership undergirds other strengths. Thus, it could be considered the "yeast" in the bread mix. Without it, other strengths would not rise to the surface.

Why Empowering Leadership Matters

Clergy face many challenges serving in high-octane leadership positions. Sharing leadership with others in the congregation helps clergy meet those challenges and at the same time effectively engages others in the mission of the congregation. Few worshipers seek out a faith community with the goal of being passive observers. In fact, as Ralph Nader observed, "the function of leadership is to produce more leaders, not more followers."[7]

The secret of clergy leadership effectiveness is the art of seeing congregants as people with great potential. Able leaders know that only when people feel "strong, capable, and efficacious" can they get extraordinary things done.[8] Great leaders see that potential and help congregants feel exceedingly valuable. Strong congregations ensure that *every* worshiper has the opportunity to be a leader and to use his or her gifts. That's how strong congregations accomplish extraordinary things!

©hris Morgan   2003

cxmedia.com

CHAPTER 10

STRENGTH 10:
LOOKING TO THE FUTURE

When our heritage is known and honored our identity is strengthened. Traditionalism, however, is an unhealthy way to relate to the past. Traditionalism dictates that nothing can change. . . . Traditionalism prays to the God who was helpful in ages past but opposes the God who is the hope for years to come. Tradition is the foundation upon which we can move faithfully into God's future.[1]

ANTHONY G. PAPPAS

What could be more important than a vision for the future? A basketball team had no gym for home games. A makeshift practice gym in a dingy building doubled as a bingo hall. One basketball hoop was bolted to an antiquated balcony. The other hoop was mounted on wheels anchored by discarded radiators. How did St. Anthony High School, Jersey City, New Jersey, win eighty-three games, and lose only five over three years, and rise to the rank of number one in the country? Obviously, the team's success was not in its facilities and equipment, but in Coach Bub Hurley's vision and the consequent desire of his players to excel. Hurley quipped, "You tell me I don't have a gym. I say we have a great record on the road."[2] Likewise, what congregations accomplish or fail to achieve is more often controlled by their vision of what they *can do* than by their internal circumstances or their community context.

The Best Years Are Ahead

The final strength we uncovered in American congregations is an orientation toward the future rather than a tendency to look back on the past. Four elements captured the extent to which congregations were focusing on the future (see Figure 10.1). More than half of worshipers in the typical congregation believe their congregation is always ready to try something new. An almost equally large number (42%) in an average congregation feel their place of worship has a clear vision, goals, and/or direction for its ministry and are strongly committed to them. But only three in ten are hopeful that the congregation

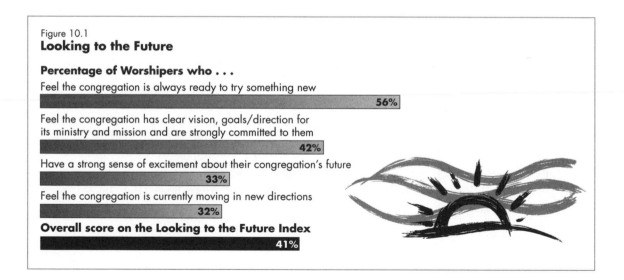

Figure 10.1
Looking to the Future

Percentage of Worshipers who . . .

Feel the congregation is always ready to try something new
56%

Feel the congregation has clear vision, goals/direction for its ministry and mission and are strongly committed to them
42%

Have a strong sense of excitement about their congregation's future
33%

Feel the congregation is currently moving in new directions
32%

Overall score on the Looking to the Future Index
41%

is currently moving in new directions. Likewise, only three in ten have a strong sense of excitement about their congregation's future.

The Looking to the Future Index

The four elements shown in Figure 10.1 comprise the Looking to the Future Index—a measure of how much worshipers are stakeholders in their congregation's future. The average score on the index is 41%.

Don't most congregations have a stake in their future? Obviously, yes, but not all congregations are equally focused on the possibilities tomorrow might bring. The scores on the index fell within about 13 percentage points on either side of the average congregational score of 41%. About half of the strengths we've discussed vary *more* across all congregations than the strength of Looking to the Future. And about half of the strengths presented vary *less* among all congregations. Thus, Looking to the Future is one aspect of congregational life where congregations are "typically" different.[3]

MYTH TRAP #10

Congregations look to the future only when the future looks promising.

Congregations of all sizes and shapes focus on the future to about the same degree. Small congregations are just as optimistic about what lies ahead as any other size congregation. But each congregation has a past that could be seen as dictating their future. As a result, congregations with a younger age profile and more new people are more likely to be looking forward.

Beyond-the-Ordinary Congregations

What do congregations that are super-focused on their future have in common?[4] Congregations scoring in the top 20% on the Looking to the Future Index are more likely to have worshipers who.

1. Have a strong sense of belonging to the congregation (Strength 4)

2. Have empowering congregational leaders (Strength 9)

3. Have begun attending the congregation in the last five years (Strength 8)

New worshipers are unencumbered by the congregation's past and likely to be more open to what the future might hold. Thus, congregations with high percentages of new worshipers have an advantage in directing the stakeholders' attention to what lies ahead. Worshipers invested in the future feel a sense of belonging because they know they are part of the future plan. Finally, empowering leaders convince worshipers that no matter how effective the congregation may have been in its mission in the past, the greatest contributions of this faith community are ahead.

Does Congregational Size Matter?

Congregations of all sizes focus on the future to about the same degree. Those of different sizes have similar scores on the Looking to the Future Index. But scores on the overall index mask some important differences between congregations on some of the elements that comprise the index. Worshipers in larger congregations are more excited about their congregation's future and more likely to believe it is currently moving in new directions than worshipers in small congregations (fewer than 100 people in worship). But worshipers in small congregations are more likely than those in large congregations to claim their church or parish has a clear vision to which they are committed. Defining a mission or vision is a different task than moving ahead in new directions. Perhaps what distinguishes large congregations from small ones is their greater willingness to act and take risks to move into the future.

Does Congregational Theology Matter?

Does theology influence how congregations think about the future? The previous chapters reveal a consistent pattern: conservative Protestant and historically black denomination churches exhibit greater strength on many of our measures than Catholic parishes or mainline Protestant churches. Thus, it is not surprising that once again conservative Protestant and historically black denomination churches have Looking to the Future as a strength (see Figure 10.2). Regardless of denomination, congregations focused on the future are more likely to build real strengths in the present.

What Else Matters?

Congregations with a younger age profile are much more likely to be focused on the future than those with an older age profile.[5] Certainly, younger worshipers are more hopeful in general and their future has a longer trajectory. But older worshipers may wish to leave a legacy by ensuring a bright future for the next generation. It would seem

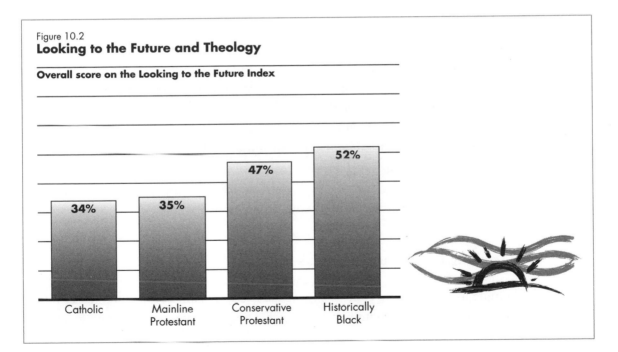

Figure 10.2
Looking to the Future and Theology

Overall score on the Looking to the Future Index

34% Catholic

35% Mainline Protestant

47% Conservative Protestant

52% Historically Black

WHAT MATTERS FOR LOOKING TO THE FUTURE?		WHO EXCELS?
Congregational size . . . . No		
Theology . . . . Yes	→	Conservative Protestant and historically black denomination churches
Age profile of worshipers . . . . Yes	→	Younger than average
Not related to numerical growth		

congregations with an older age profile would be more concerned about what lies ahead for their congregation, but this does not appear to be the case.

Will Looking to the Future Help Us Grow in Numbers?

Now we have the flavor and power of all ten congregational strengths in our recipe. What kind of ingredient is an orientation toward the future for predicting numerical growth in congregations? When the power of all the other strengths is taken into account, the strength of Looking to the Future recedes into the background.[6] It is not directly responsible for helping congregations grow. In fact, it may be possible that a future orientation is stimulated by growth. But as we've argued in previous chapters, this strength is part of the web that makes congregations strong. Looking to the Future provides motivation for leaders to empower others and for worshipers to get more involved.

Why Looking to the Future Matters

The heroine in the romantic comedy *My Big Fat Greek Wedding* complained to her future groom that her huge Greek family was somewhat overcontrolling and irritating at times.

His response to his future bride was classic advice: "Don't let your past dictate who you are, but let it become part of who you become."

All congregations have obstacles in their present and past that distract them from what the future holds. Congregations building on their present and past strengths use them as foundations for becoming who God is calling them to be.

Strength by Strength

Doing what is best does not require great strength. But great strength is required to choose the best path.

We plead guilty to positive thinking.[1] We see abundant reasons for hopefulness about the future of American congregations. At the same time, we are painfully aware of obstacles that lie in their paths. We agree with the view that "Our society will be defined not only by what we create, but by what we refuse to destroy."[2] One obstacle is the incredible number of small congregations (56%) with fewer than 100 in worship attendance. Both small and large congregations are often resistant to change that over the long haul moves them more toward life than toward death. Yet they all demonstrate strengths. The previous chapters uncovered many areas where small congregations excel. We believe we can find ways to help them build on those strengths. Isn't refusing to allow their demise at least as important as any other task for people of faith?

How do we refuse to allow congregations to shrink in size and effectiveness? What can we offer to aid them in becoming resilient and growing congregations? We discovered ten qualities that are evident in strong congregations. This book has outlined in detail the dimensions and intensity of these qualities in strong and beyond-the-ordinary congregations. The next step is yours—a courageous conversation about what God calls congregations to do. What stands in your way?

The Knowing-Doing Gap

Listening to the experiences of many congregations over a number of years revealed a phenomenon that puzzled us. When congregations receive good information about themselves and their surrounding communities, they sometimes fail to use it. Why didn't this good information lead to positive change in real congregations? One possible answer has been called the "knowing-doing gap." In business organizations, for example, managers know the "best practices" for maximizing employee potential and productivity. However, managers sometimes do not use this information as they perform their jobs. One study pursued the major barriers that prevent people from turning knowledge into action. Often, leaders tend to consider *talking* about something as equivalent to actually *doing* something about it.[3] Planning for the future can be another no-action strategy. Planning doesn't produce a future unless someone *does* something. Another problem is the belief that making a decision is enough. If no additional attention is given to ensuring the decision is implemented, the decision withers and dies. Other substitutes for action include making presentations, preparing documents, and writing mission statements.[4]

Another stumbling block for moving ahead to action is the *way* we talk. We ascribe status to those who use complex language, ideas, and processes. Yet *simple talk* is "more likely to lead to action."[5] A simple idea, strategy, or philosophy is more difficult to misunderstand or misrepresent. Simple language rubs against the allure of complexity. Many of us have bought the old adage, "If the solution were simple, we would have already thought of it."[6] We assert that if you don't understand the simple language of strengths, you're a traveler who left the map at home.

The Lion's Share: Courageous Conversations

Another reason behind inaction is our reluctance to have necessary conversations. All of us put off discussions or conversations that are difficult, or unpleasant, or that have unpredictable outcomes. Differences of opinion surface in every area of our life. The more important the issue in our lives, the more difficult it is to hold a conversation that may or may not clear the air.

The authors of *Difficult Conversations*, a book about discussing what matters most, say that "each difficult conversation is really three conversations."[7] The first part of a difficult conversation is the description of "what happened." It should be easy to objectively describe what took place, but it's not. For example, two people agree to meet for dinner. One person shows up at the agreed-upon meeting place and ends up waiting for thirty minutes. By the time the second person appears, a difficult conversation is brewing. The first person to arrive charges the second person with being rudely late. The second person accuses the first person of being mistaken—the meeting time was scheduled thirty minutes later than the first person thought it was. Who is right? It really doesn't matter because the two can't agree on what actually happened.

The second part of a difficult conversation is the "feelings conversation." Hard conversations generate feelings. "What you said made me angry." Anxiety, hurt, fear, resentment, and scores of other emotions bubble to the surface as we attempt to sort things out between us.

The third part of a difficult conversation is the "identity conversation." This thorny conversation takes place inside of us as a debate about what this exchange is all about. Each of us has a self-image that includes qualities such as thoughtfulness, competency, being lovable, or being a good person. The difficult conversation calls into question whether our core identity is true. None of us enjoys questioning how we *like* to think of ourselves.

How is understanding difficult conversations relevant to congregational life? Through our research we hope we've made a contribution to helping congregational leaders learn "what is happening here." An accurate description of current worshipers, strengths of the congregation, and up-to-date knowledge about the surrounding community go a long way toward moving congregations to purposeful action. But something seems to prevent congregations from using objective descriptions of "who they are" to become "who they want to be." A difficult congregational conversation is needed. Leaders and worshipers must assimilate the reality that the new and accurate information provides. This first part of a difficult congregational conversation draws upon the congregation's mind—their rational and analytical skills. Getting everyone on the "same page" or same perception of reality is an essential first step toward action.

The second part of a difficult congregational conversation—acute feelings about the situation at hand—should also take place in congregations. However, this part of the conversation is less likely to be openly discussed than the "what happened" aspect. How do we feel about what this new information says about who we are? We may not be doing as well as we'd like to be in caring for children and youth in the congregation. How do we feel about it? Discouraged or resigned? Challenged or excited about new possibilities? Feelings that are not put on the table and openly addressed are present in the room anyway. Screening feelings out of a conversation does more harm than good. Feelings affect future action as much as a clear understanding of what is objectively happening within the congregation. If we fail to resolve how we feel about what is currently happening in our congregation, action is unlikely. Having a difficult conversation that includes feelings taps into the congregation's heart—the source of imaginative solutions and creative strategies.

The third aspect of difficult congregational conversations, which deals with our identity, takes effort to give it voice. We may not be aware of how new information or suggestions for change "hook" our core congregational identity. We might be a "tall-steeple" church—one of the largest in our denomination—and assume we're the "best" in everything. Or perhaps our congregation is known for its community ministry. What happens if we learn we could be doing better in some areas? What if new information challenges these beliefs? If it contradicts our core identity, we are likely to reject the new information or resist changing to accommodate it. Having a difficult conversation that challenges a congregation's identity calls for courage because it may collide with worshipers' core beliefs.

Congregational conversations that include all aspects of a difficult conversation—reality, feelings, and identity—lead to action. A congregational identity grounded in reality and feelings moves a congregation to an authentic and enduring response. Strong congregations take risks and try new ways of doing things. They take heart in the adage that "if at first you don't succeed, you're about average." Nevertheless, they keep experimenting until something works for them. Congregations that regularly engage in coura-geous conversations are more likely to find themselves in the right place: "The place God calls you to is the place where your deep gladness and the world's deep hunger meet."[8]

Closing the knowing-doing gap and engaging in difficult conversations about con-gregational life do not guarantee action either. No doubt other factors shorten the reach of congregations seeking to become stronger in mission. For some congregations, the reality of declining numbers of worshipers foreshadows any effort for greater effective-ness. Are strong congregations also growing numerically by attracting new worshipers?

What about Numerical Growth?

We do *not* believe that numerical growth is the best barometer for determining whether a congregation is strong and healthy. We assert that the ten congregational strengths identified through our research are more important than numbers for understanding congregations of various sizes, types, and locations. However, we also recognize that many congregations struggle with declining membership and resources. For such a con-gregation this reality often looms larger than most other issues. Like the old saying that "money is not important to human happiness unless you don't have any," numerical growth does *not* make a strong congregation, but continued numerical decline will even-tually crush a congregation's ability to exhibit any kind of strength. For many congrega-tions, understanding some of the dynamics of growth can destroy useless myths, reduce wasted efforts, and enhance the investment of time and money.

We examined the impact of sixteen factors on numerical growth. These sixteen fac-tors included the ten strengths, as well as six other factors that many believe influence congregational growth: congregational size, average age of worshipers, average income of worshipers, percentage of worshipers who are female, theology/faith group of the con-gregation, and population growth in the zip code where the congregation is located.

Three congregational strengths are positive predictors of numerical growth: Caring for Children and Youth, Participating in the Congregation, and Welcoming New People. In short, congregations growing in numbers also have higher scores on these three indices. Substantive comments about these important relationships are contained in the preceding chapters.

Knowing what is *not* a cause of growth is just as important as knowing what is. A number of factors are *not* related to the numerical growth of congregations. As the following list shows, four out of the ten congregational strengths do not predict numerical growth, and the six other causes often declared critical predictors of numerical gain are not related to growth. When all sixteen factors are taken into account, the following were unrelated to numerical growth:

- Strength 2: Meaningful Worship

- Strength 4: Having a Sense of Belonging

- Strength 9: Empowering Leadership

- Strength 10: Looking to the Future

- The size of the congregation

- The average age of worshipers in the congregation

- The average income of worshipers in the congregation

- The percentage of female worshipers in the congregation

- The theology of the congregation (e.g., mainline Protestant)

- Local population growth

Much to our surprise, three congregational strengths are negative predictors of numerical growth: Growing Spiritually, Focusing on the Community, and Sharing Faith. This means congregations doing well on these strengths are usually declining numerically. We've provided substantive discussion of these findings in previous chapters. But here is one part of the answer about why these negative relationships exist: Congregations currently doing well in one of the three areas listed above tend to be *below average* on several other strengths that are important for congregational growth (e.g., Caring for Children and Youth). Our findings are *descriptions* of the current mix of strengths possessed by American congregations. We are not *prescribing* the way congregations should operate. Congregations can be Growing Spiritually and growing numerically, for example. Just because many present congregations have this constellation of strengths does not dictate what the future holds for American congregations.

Does Size, Theology, or the Age Profile of the Congregation Matter?

Congregational size matters for six out of the ten strengths we presented in previous chapters (see appendix 4). But the size of a congregation doesn't always relate to a congregational strength in the expected way. In five areas small congregations excel—Growing Spiritually, Participating in the Congregation, Having a Sense of Belonging, Sharing Faith, and Empowering Leadership. Our findings confirm the observations of Phil Stevenson: "Check your health, not your attendance sheet. Check your heart, not your numbers. Nothing can grow indefinitely. An elephant gets to a certain size and stops growing. A mouse grows and stops. They are not the same size, but they are healthy."[9]

Theology, as reflected by denomination or faith group, is associated with all ten strengths (see appendix 5). Conservative Protestant and/or historically black denomination churches outdistance the other two denominational families—mainline Protestants and Catholics—on nine out of the ten strengths. What strength is the exception? Mainline Protestant churches excel on the Focusing on the Community strength. Certainly, we don't advocate that congregations change their core beliefs and traditions. However, our hope is that leaders will develop strategies for building on congregational strengths based on tradition—honoring the best from the past, rather than traditionalism—undeviating allegiance to ineffective past practices.[10]

Congregations whose worshipers are younger than the average age in other congregations gather more strength in four areas—Having a Sense of Belonging, Caring for Children and Youth, Welcoming New People, and Looking to the Future (see appendix 6). Congregations with older-than-average worshipers can boast of Focusing on the Community as a more common strength. With only five strengths related to the congregational age profile, this feature of a congregation is the least important among the three we explored (size of the congregation, theology, and age profile of the congregation's worshipers).

Theology is a solid predictor of all ten congregational strengths. Congregational size is a less powerful predictor, having a direct impact on six of the ten strengths. Age is least robust, influencing five of the ten strengths. If you could know only one thing about a congregation, its denominational affiliation or faith group would help you the most in predicting its strengths. Congregations live the values that stem from their theological views. Congregations do not live the goals they set for themselves or their visions for the future unless those goals and visions are rooted in their core beliefs.

How Much Are Congregations Alike?

The range and richness of congregational life deserves the best-detailed description. We were awed by the variety of religious communities and learned from their experiences. Yet we also found that broad patterns exist in this detailed mosaic—ten strengths appeared again and again in innumerable combinations. How are congregations most alike in terms of the strengths we uncovered? Three strengths pop out as the most common expressions of congregational life. In other words, congregations tend to look alike when we see these strengths in the real world. The range between congregations doing the best and congregations doing the worst on these strengths was not large.

First, congregations are alike in the way worshipers describe the worship services (see Figure 11.1). Worshipers tend to be similarly satisfied across congregations. We know that the worship services in all these congregations cannot possibly be the same "quality," but worshipers report the same levels of satisfaction nonetheless. This finding challenges congregational leaders. Knowing the congregation is meeting the spiritual needs of current worshipers is only half the battle. When we recognize that the majority of Americans are not attending or participating in a faith community, the challenge becomes clear. We must admit that as "insiders" we cannot be objective about our own worship services and cannot judge how people in the community might experience them.

Figure 11.1
Coefficient of Relative Variation

Strength	Mean	Standard Deviation	CRV	Rank
1. Growing Spiritually	47.35	10.88	0.23	8
2. Meaningful Worship	62.03	11.38	0.18	10
3. Participating in the Congregation	60.08	13.44	0.22	9
4. Having a Sense of Belonging	36.53	11.37	0.31	5
5. Caring for Children and Youth	50.05	12.46	0.25	7
6. Focusing on the Community	32.88	8.93	0.27	6
7. Sharing Faith	32.23	14.63	0.45	2
8. Welcoming New People	33.26	17.37	0.52	1
9. Empowering Leadership	49.25	15.92	0.32	3
10. Looking to the Future	40.82	13.18	0.32	3

Note: The CRV is calculated as the standard deviation divided by the mean. This statistic makes it possible to compare indices that have different standard deviations and means. See appendix 2 for more information.

Rank: 1 = Greatest diversity among congregations; where congregations are most different
       10 = Least diversity among congregations; where congregations are most alike

A second way congregations tend to be alike is in their ability to engage worshipers in activities of the congregation beyond attending services. Again, the range between the highest and lowest scores is fairly small. This may be a norm of American religious behavior—participating in a congregation and attending worship services is enough to "mark" someone as "religious." Since a minority of the population currently attends worship services, congregational participation of any type clearly distinguishes people of faith from the rest of the community. It is this distinction that is perhaps more important than the distinction between worshipers having greater or lesser participation in their congregation. Worshipers who are very involved in their congregations are part of a small subculture specific to their faith tradition.

How does this relatively small range of congregational participation scores play out? Congregational leaders who are unaware that roughly half of worshipers have only surface-level involvement can be discouraged by the experiences of their congregation. They can take comfort in the fact that the majority of congregations are in the same boat. Yet broader involvement in congregational life by worshipers is a worthwhile goal for many reasons.

A third way congregations are more alike than they are different is in their spiritual growth. Worshipers in most congregations tend to describe their spiritual growth in much the same ways. Probably some congregations have a higher bar than others. But worshipers take their cues from others and from the culture of their congregation. They get the "message" about what constitutes a faithful life and growing commitment and judge themselves accordingly *in their context.*

In What Ways Are Congregations Different?

Congregations are most different when it comes to the percentage of new people (those who started participating sometime in the last five years) they find in their midst. The range on this strength is greater than any other. Some congregations have few new participants—fewer than one in ten are new in the last five years. Other congregations have numerous newcomers—two out of three people in the pew have arrived in the last five years. What a difference this fact makes in the life of the congregation! For example, when two out of three people are new, institutional memory is quite limited. New ways of doing things may be adopted on a regular basis, leading to a sense of instability. But obviously the positives are great, too—new interest, resources, and growth. Those who are new in a setting where newcomers are a small minority experience something else. They may *never* feel like they fully belong. They may believe they'll be seen as outsiders or newcomers for years and years to come.

Another way congregations differ is how and when their worshipers share their faith. In some congregations, worshipers often invite others to worship services and other activities. In other congregations, worshipers rarely do so. Some congregations are filled with worshipers who feel at ease talking about their faith and its meaning in their lives. But in other congregations worshipers are reluctant to do so—perhaps because they believe their life speaks for itself.

The third way congregations diverge has to do with leadership. Some congregations have empowering leadership, and others are served by leaders who use different styles. It's not surprising that a range of styles exists in today's congregations. Scores of current church leadership books present contradictory views about the most effective role and style of the leader—directive or proactive; visionary leadership at all costs; reactive; consensus builders; and so the list goes. Given no evidence about what works best in which situations, leaders devise a strategy based on their theology, training, and experience.

The remaining strengths fall in the middle between the first group of strengths where scores are fairly similar—Meaningful Worship, Participating in the Congregation, and Growing Spiritually—and the group of strengths where considerable diversity was found—Welcoming New People, Sharing Faith, and Empowering Leadership. Congregational scores on the remaining four areas of congregational life have an "average" spread: Having a Sense of Belonging, Looking to the Future, Focusing on the Community, and Caring for Children and Youth.

Strong Congregations Become Beyond-the-Ordinary Congregations

The previous ten chapters revealed the strengths that predict which congregations are likely to rise to the top 20% of all congregations on any given strength. Figure 11.2 graphically displays all of those relationships. A quick glance shows how interwoven the ten congregational strengths are. For example, high scores on Strength 10, Looking to the Future, are predicted by three other strengths—Having a Sense of Belonging, Welcoming New People, and Empowering Leadership (summarized by looking down the last column). That means congregations in the top 20% on Looking to the Future are also likely to have high scores on the other three strengths.

Figure 11.2 also shows that Strength 10, Looking to the Future, predicts many other strengths (seen by looking horizontally across the row for Looking to the Future). This strength helps to predict strength in five other areas (Strengths 3, 4, 5, 8, and 9).

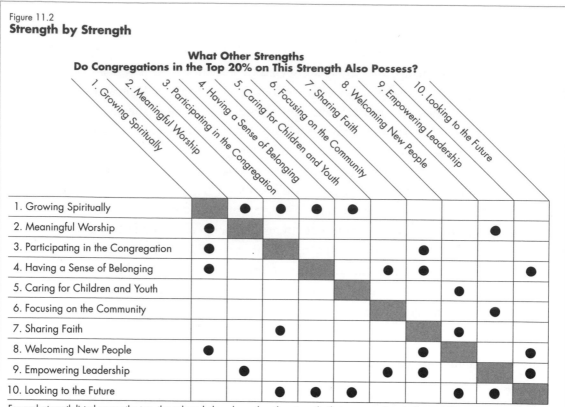

Figure 11.2
Strength by Strength

What Other Strengths Do Congregations in the Top 20% on This Strength Also Possess?

For each strength listed across the top, the column below shows the other strengths that congregations in the top 20% on that strength also possess. For example, congregations in the top 20% on Growing Spiritually also tend to score high on Meaningful Worship, Participating in the Congregation, Having a Sense of Belonging, and Welcoming New People.

Based on logistic regression comparing congregations in the top 20% on the strength at the top of the column to other congregations.

Looking to the Future is the winner in terms of how frequently it pushes congregations into the extraordinary category in one or more of the other nine strengths.

Three other strengths—Growing Spiritually, Having a Sense of Belonging, and Empowering Leadership—are also key players in beyond-the-ordinary congregations by supporting four additional strengths each. Viewing Figure 11.2 horizontally reveals these relationships. Growing Spiritually supports Strengths 2, 3, 4, and 5; Having a Sense of

Belonging supports Strengths 1, 6, 7, and 10; and Empowering Leadership supports Strengths 2, 6, 7, and 10. Welcoming New People fosters vitality in three other strengths (Strengths 1, 7, and 10). Meaningful Worship, Participating in the Congregation, and Sharing Faith lend support to two strengths each—Meaningful Worship: Strengths 1 and 9; Participating in the Congregation: Strengths 1 and 7; and Sharing Faith: Strengths 3 and 8. Finally, Caring for Children and Youth (Strength 8) and Focusing on the Community (Strength 9) each supports only one other strength.

What about That Wizard?

The road to congregational strength requires mind, heart, and courage. The three *Wizard of Oz* characters illustrating these qualities—the Scarecrow, the Tin Woodman, and the Cowardly Lion—encountered two others on their journey. Do the Wizard and Dorothy represent anything of value for congregations striving to reach beyond the ordinary?

The Wizard in the Land of Oz symbolizes the magical trump-card approach. In the end, Dorothy and her friends saw behind the curtain, glimpsing the king of the one-trick illusion. They realized how little power for change and hope for the future the Wizard actually offered. Congregations are also offered trump-card approaches—"focus on congregational size to be successful and strong"; "change your worship style"; "get the best leader"; "identify your core mission"; "pinpoint your Achilles heel or weakest area"; and "move out to the growing suburbs." Strong congregations see what's behind the curtain and choose something more valuable instead.

Congregational life is not simple. Our research demonstrates that all congregations have strengths. Further, congregations require multiple strengths to be effective. A congregation that excels in serving the community but lacks any other strength is little more than a social service agency. A congregation that excels in providing a sense of belonging where people care for one another but lacks other strengths is little more than a social club. A congregation that excels in caring for their children but lacks any other strength is little more than a day-care center. Congregations must focus on multiple strengths to do all that is required of people of faith. Any attempt to advise congregations without taking into account the complexity of their essence is ill advice.

Who Is Dorothy?

Dorothy is the champion who encourages the others to continue traveling the yellow brick road. She reassures them that the trip is worth it and reminds them that they are not mere tourists but pilgrims. Dorothy is the inquirer, supportively waiting for the answers that keep her companions traveling. Even when they're fearful because they've pulled back the curtain and exposed their limitations, she remains confident about the future. She embodies the qualities of wisdom, heart, and courage—she is hope.[11]

In our story, God takes this role. As our companion and friend, God comforts us with the promises of an ancient prayer, Psalm 138:

> You answered when we called.
> You built up strength within us.
> You will do everything you have promised us.
> Complete the work you have begun.[12]

U.S. Congregational
Life Survey Methodology

Over 300,000 worshipers in more than 2,000 congregations across America participated in the U.S. Congregational Life Survey—making it the largest survey of worshipers in America ever conducted. Three types of surveys were completed in each participating congregation: (a) an attendee survey completed by all worshipers age fifteen and older who attended worship services during the weekend of April 29, 2001; (b) a Congregational Profile describing the congregation's facilities, staff, programs, and worship services completed by one person in the congregation; and (c) a Leader Survey completed by the pastor, priest, minister, rabbi, or other leader. Together the information collected provides a unique three-dimensional look at religious life in America.

The National Opinion Research Center (NORC) at the University of Chicago identified a random sample of U.S. congregations attended by individuals who participated in the General Social Survey (GSS) in the year 2000. All GSS participants who reported that they attended worship at least once in the prior year were asked to name the place where they worshiped. Since the GSS involves a national random sample of individuals, congregations identified by GSS participants comprise a national random sample of congregations. NORC researchers verified that each nominated congregation was an actual congregation and then invited each congregation to participate in the project. Of 1,214 nominated and verified congregations, 807 agreed to participate (66%), and 434 returned completed surveys from their worshipers (36%). (A wide variety of reasons were given by congregations that chose not to participate.) Worshipers in these congregations, representing all 50 states, completed 122,043 attendee surveys, which are the primary source of the findings reported here. The size of this scientific statistical sample far exceeds the size of most national surveys. Studies designed to provide a representative profile of adults living in the United States typically include about 1,000 people.

Denominations were also invited and encouraged to draw a random sample of their congregations. Denominational samples were large enough so that the results are representative of worshipers and congregations in each denomination. This allows denominations to compare their "typical" congregation and worshiper to congregations and worshipers in other denominations. Denominations participating in this oversampling procedure were: Church of the Nazarene, Evangelical Lutheran Church in America (ELCA), Presbyterian Church (U.S.A.), Roman Catholic Church, Seventh-day Adventist Church, Southern Baptist Convention, United Methodist Church (UMC), and United Church of Christ (UCC). Results from these oversamples are not included here.

Additional information about the methods used in this study are available on our Web site: www.uscongregations.org.

QUESTIONS AND ANSWERS

What level of analysis was used?

Most of the information presented in our book, *A Field Guide to U.S. Congregations,* was based on surveys completed by worshipers (individual-level analyses). That is, we examined the responses of individual worshipers in preparing that book. We discussed who worshipers are, what they are doing in their congregations, how they're involved in the community, and what they see for the future of the congregation. To write *this* book, we've aggregated the responses of individual worshipers to the congregational level (congregational-level analyses). That is, responses from all worshipers in each congregation have been combined to allow us the opportunity to see what they say as a group about their congregation. Here we investigate what makes congregations strong. We also weighted the congregational-level data to account for size and non-response biases. Because congregations were nominated for participation in this study by a random sample of adults, larger congregations (with so many more worshipers) were more likely to have been nominated. The statistical weights we used counterbalanced this bias. Similarly, certain denominations and faith groups were underrepresented in the sample, and the weights also corrected for this bias. (Because of these differences, unweighted worshiper-level figures presented in the first book may not match the weighted congregational-level data presented here.)

Both books include some results from information that was provided on the Congregational Profile—the survey completed by one person in each congregation describing the congregation's programs, services, facilities, staff, and finances.

How were the ten strengths identified?

In the first book, we examined congregations and their worshipers in four interrelated areas—Spiritual Connections, Inside Connections, Outside Connections, and Identity Connections. The ten strengths in this book flow from those four areas and tap the essential strengths of congregations. We believe that all congregations possess strengths, and this multifaceted approach allows congregations to find the areas in which they excel. Also, we're indebted to many congregational and denominational leaders, church consultants, and religious researchers who helped us inventory the characteristics of healthy and vital congregations.

How were the questions that make up each strength selected?

We used a systematic method to determine the specific questions that make up each strength. First, we listed all survey questions that were designed to measure each strength. Second, we selected for inclusion in the measure the specific answers to each question that were most important. For example, when using the question about worshipers' private devotions, two answers were chosen because they are most reflective of growth in faith—spending time in private devotional activities either "every day or most days" or "a few times a week." Third, we subjected this pool of questions and specific answers for each strength to statistical analyses that allowed us to determine those combinations that do the best job of measuring that strength. We used Cronbach's coefficient alpha statistic (a measure of the reliability of a scale) to make this determination. The higher the number, the more reliable the scale. Sometimes, questions that we thought would be important in measuring a particular strength turned out to relatively unimportant and were eliminated from the analyses. Cronbach's alpha for each strength is shown here:

Growing Spiritually Index	0.77
Meaningful Worship Index	0.86
Participating in the Congregation Index	0.82
Sense of Belonging Index	0.74
Caring for Children and Youth Index	0.65
Focusing on the Community Index	0.81
Sharing Faith Index	0.90
Welcoming New People Index	**
Empowering Leadership Index	0.84
Looking to the Future Index	0.82

**A Cronbach's alpha could not be calculated for the Welcoming New People Index because this index was based on a single survey item (i.e., the percentage of worshipers who began participating in the last five years).

How are overall scores calculated?

The overall score for each strength is calculated as the average (mean) of the questions that comprise that strength. The overall scores reported here are the averages of the means from all congregations that participated. We also calculated an overall score for each congregation using the answers of all worshipers who completed surveys there.

Can I compare the scores across strengths?

No. Because the questions that comprise each index use widely different scales, they cannot be compared. That is, just because the average score on the Growing Spiritually Index is higher than the average score on the Meaningful Worship Index does *not* mean that congregations in general are doing better in the area of spirituality than in the area of worship. It *is* appropriate to compare the scores of different types of congregations on one index—for example, comparing large congregations to small ones on the Growing

Spiritually Index. Using percentile scores (see below), an individual congregation can see how its scores on each index compare to the national average for each index.

How were the denominational families established?

The five denominational families used in this book represent a common typology of congregations used by religion researchers. Congregations within each family are fairly similar to one another in terms of theology and belief, and they are less similar to congregations in other faith groups. Appendix 3 shows the specific denominations participating in the U.S. Congregational Life Survey that fall in each category.

How are differences by congregational size or faith group or age determined?

A two-step process was used to look for differences across congregational size, faith group, and age. First, an analysis of variance (ANOVA) was used to look for overall differences. When the ANOVA revealed a statistically significant difference (that is, a difference large enough that it would occur by chance fewer than five times in 100), the second step involved using the Games-Howell statistical test. Games-Howell shows which specific groups differ from other groups in the sample.

What is a percentile?

A percentile score describes your congregation's position within a rank-order distribution of all congregations. It indicates the percent of cases falling below your score. When a pediatrician tells you that your two-week-old infant weighs 10 pounds, 6 ounces, and falls in the ninety-second percentile for weight, you know that your child weighs more than 92% of all other two-week-old children. We focus on congregations in the eightieth percentile or above on each strength because they go beyond the ordinary. Their scores are above those of 80% of other congregations on a strength index and are particularly worthy of our interest.

What is the Coefficient of Relative Variation (CRV)?

The CRV is a useful statistic for comparing two scores (or in our case, indices) that have substantially different standard deviations and means. The formula is simply the standard deviation divided by the mean. Because distributions with higher average scores tend to have higher standard deviations, the CRV adjusts for this characteristic. For example, the Meaningful Worship Index average score is 62%, considerably higher than the Focusing on the Community Index score of 33%. The standard deviations of these two indices vary as well (i.e., 11.38 vs. 8.93). The CRV allows us to compare the ten strength indices across congregations to determine how much congregations are different and how much they are alike (see Figure 11.1).

How was congregational growth measured?

Each participating congregation completed a Congregational Profile that asked for the average annual worship attendance for the last five years (1996 to 2001). Because the survey was given in April 2001, worship attendance figures for that year were incomplete, and a number of congregations did not report that figure. Growth was measured as an average annual percentage of growth or decline in worship attendance between 1996 and 2000 (attendance in 2000 minus attendance in 1996, the difference divided by attendance in 1996) and as a percentage of growth or decline between 1996 and 2001. Thus, positive numbers indicate a congregation has more worshipers in 2000 or 2001 than in 1996, and negative numbers indicate fewer worshipers. Some congregations did not report attendance figures for 1996 and/or for 2000. In such cases, growth was calculated based on the earliest and latest reported attendance figures.

How was the relationship between each of the ten strengths and congregational growth determined?

Each of the ten strengths is part of an intricate web of relationships within a congregation. In order to explore these relationships we employed a statistical method that takes into account all the relationships simultaneously (i.e., multiple regression analyses). The same statistical approach is used when calculating health risks like heart disease. Some of the strongest predictors of heart disease are gender (i.e., male), age, and lifestyle (e.g., smoking, diet). These factors remain important even when other factors like education or occupation are taken into account.

Using this statistical method enabled us to predict a congregation's score on numerical growth based on scores on the ten strengths and several other congregational factors—size, theology, the percentage of female worshipers in the congregation, the age profile of worshipers, the average income of worshipers, and the community population growth rate. For example, a congregation's score on the Caring for Children and Youth Index (see chapter 5) predicts their numerical growth score. The relationship between the two scores—the Caring for Children and Youth Index and numerical growth—remains important even when factors like congregational size, theology, the percentage of female worshipers, and the age profile of the congregation are considered.

How big of a difference is needed to indicate that my congregation is different from the comparison groups?

In general, differences of 3% to 5% are considered statistically significant differences. That means that any difference less than that amount may be due entirely to random variation in the measures.

Can my congregation's scores change?

Yes. Although it is unlikely that your scores will change rapidly, as your congregation changes—for example, adds new worshipers, programs, and staff; loses former members (whether due to death, mobility, or other factors); discontinues ineffective or outdated programs; or experiences a changing financial situation—your scores will change, too. Unless there has been considerable change in your congregation, we don't recommend reassessing your scores (by retaking the survey) more often than every three to five years.

How quickly does the national picture of American congregations change?

Researchers and others agree that congregational change at the national level is much slower than at the individual congregational level. The portrait of U.S. congregations changes incrementally. Most trends are long-term, lasting for ten to twenty years or more. We believe a snapshot taken of a national random sample of congregations should detect most significant shifts in religious life among worshipers and their congregations. Our assumption is based on congregational studies conducted by other U.S. sociologists (e.g., Mark Chavez, University of Arizona) and by our research colleagues in Australia—the National Church Life Survey (NCLS). The NCLS has conducted four national surveys of Australian worshipers since 1986. In their numerous publications (see www.ncls.org.au), they carefully document steady but modest change at the national level.

My congregation would like to see how we compare with the U.S. results. Can we take the survey? Will the report help us identify our strengths?

Yes! Contact us toll-free at 1-888-728-7228, ext. 2040. Or for more information see our Web site, www.uscongregations.org. You can conduct the survey at your convenience. We'll send you all the surveys you need (forms are available in English, Spanish, and Korean), pens to complete them, and instructions for giving the survey in worship. Once your congregation completes the survey, we'll prepare customized reports and provide two videos with step-by-step instructions for interpreting the reports. You'll also receive a copy of the book *A Field Guide to U.S. Congregations* (Westminster John Knox Press, 2002), which describes the national picture from a random sample of congregations. Please contact us by phone or check the Web site for more details or to obtain information on current fees (based on the size of your congregation).

DENOMINATIONAL FAMILIES

The five denominational families used in this book represent a common typology of congregations used by religion researchers. The specific denominations participating in the U.S. Congregational Life Survey that fall in each category are shown below. Because the "other" category is so broad (including Jewish synagogues, Buddhist temples, and other non-Christian faiths), we do not report means for this group separately in the book. These "other" congregations were included in analyses used to develop the strength indices and are included in the overall scores we report, but they are excluded from the analyses by faith group. The numbers of congregations in each denominational family are: Catholic, n = 100; mainline Protestant, n = 180; conservative Protestant, n = 129; historically black denomination churches, n = 9; and other congregations, n = 12 (these numbers are unweighted).

Catholic Churches:

Roman Catholic

Mainline Protestant Churches:

American Baptist Churches in the U.S.A.
Baptist Bible Fellowship, International
Christian Church (Disciples of Christ)
Episcopal/Anglican (unspecified)
Episcopal Church
Lutheran (unspecified)
Christian Reformed Church in North
    America
Unitarian Universalist Association

Evangelical Lutheran Church in America
United Methodist Church
Unity of the Brethren (Moravian)
Greek Orthodox
Presbyterian (unspecified)
Presbyterian Church (U.S.A.)
United Church of Christ

Conservative Protestant Churches:

Seventh-day Adventist
Baptist (unspecified)
Conservative Baptist Association of America
Free Will Baptist
United Baptist
General Association of Regular
    Baptist Church
Southern Baptist Convention
Christian and Missionary Alliances
Christian Churches and Churches of Christ
Churches of Christ
Christian Churches of North America
Church of God
Church of God (Anderson, Indiana)
Church of God (Cleveland, Tennessee)
Church of the Nazarene
Conservative Congregational Christian
    Conference

Foursquare Gospel
Lutheran Church, Missouri Synod
Mennonite (unspecified)
Mennonite Church
Free Methodist Church of North America
Missionary
Pentecostal (unspecified)
Assemblies of God
United Pentecostal Church, International
Presbyterian Church in America
Unity School of Christianity
Wesleyan Church
Non-denominational
Non-denominational Evangelical
Non-denominational Pentecostal

Historically Black Denomination Churches:

National Baptist Convention, USA
Church of God in Christ

African Methodist Episcopal Zion Church

Other Congregations:

Buddhist Communities
Judaism (unspecified)
Conservative Judaism
Reform Judaism

Church of Jesus Christ of Latter-day
    Saints
Reorganized Church of Jesus Christ of
    Latter-day Saints
Non-denominational, Non-Christian

STRENGTHS BY CONGREGATIONAL SIZE

Strength	Small	Mid-Size	Large
1. Growing Spiritually	● ● ●	● ●	●
2. Meaningful Worship	● ● ●	●	● ●
3. Participating in the Congregation	● ● ●	● ●	●
4. Having a Sense of Belonging	● ● ●	● ●	●
5. Caring for Children and Youth	●	● ● ●	● ●
6. Focusing on the Community	●	● ● ●	●
7. Sharing Faith	● ● ●	● ●	●
8. Welcoming New People	●	●	● ● ●
9. Empowering Leadership	● ● ●	● ●	●
10. Looking to the Future	●	● ● ●	● ●

Small = fewer than 100 in worship   Mid-size = 100–350 in worship   Large = more than 350 in worship

● = lowest average score   ● ● ● = highest average score (shaded)

Bold text indicates a statistically significant overall difference (Strengths 1, 3, 4, 5, 7, and 9 show significant overall differences).

STRENGTHS BY DENOMINATIONAL FAMILY

Strength	Catholic	Mainline Protestant	Conservative Protestant	Historically Black
1. Growing Spiritually	●●	●●	●●●●	●●●●
2. Meaningful Worship	●●	●	●●●●	●●●
3. Participating in the Congregation	●	●●	●●●	●●●●
4. Having a Sense of Belonging	●	●●	●●●	●●●●
5. Caring for Children and Youth	●	●●	●●●●	●●●●
6. Focusing on the Community	●●	●●●●●	●	●●●
7. Sharing Faith	●	●●	●●●	●●●●
8. Welcoming New People	●●	●●●	●●●●	●
9. Empowering Leadership	●	●●	●●●●	●●●
10. Looking to the Future	●	●●	●●●	●●●●

Catholic = Roman Catholic
Mainline Protestant = Methodist, Presbyterian, Lutheran, Episcopal, United Church of Christ, etc.
Conservative Protestant = Baptist, Seventh-day Adventist, Assemblies of God, Nazarenes, Pentecostal, etc.
Historically Black Denomination = National Baptist Convention, Church of God in Christ, African Methodist Episcopal Zion, etc.

● = lowest average score
●●●● = highest average score (shaded)
Note that for Strengths 1 and 5 conservative Protestant and historically black churches have tied for the highest scores.

Bold text indicates a statistically significant overall difference (all show statistically significant overall differences).

STRENGTHS BY AVERAGE AGE IN THE CONGREGATION

Strength	Younger	Older
1. Growing Spiritually	● ●	●
2. Meaningful Worship	●	●
3. Participating in the Congregation	●	● ●
4. Having a Sense of Belonging	● ●	●
5. Caring for Children and Youth	● ●	●
6. Focusing on the Community	●	● ●
7. Sharing Faith	● ●	●
8. Welcoming New People	● ●	●
9. Empowering Leadership	●	●
10. Looking to the Future	● ●	●

Younger = congregations with an average age less than or equal to 52
  Older = congregations with an average age above 52

● = lowest average score
● ● = highest average score (shaded)
  Note that for Strengths 2 and 9 there is no difference between the two groups, so each is marked with ● and no shading is shown.

Bold text indicates a statistically significant overall difference (Strengths 4, 5, 6, 8, and 10 show statistically significant differences).

THE INTERNATIONAL CONGREGATIONAL LIFE SURVEY

The International Congregational Life Survey (ICLS) was initiated in 1999 as a collaborative effort of four countries. Extending the National Church Life Survey (NCLS) used earlier in Australia, the aim is to provide mission resources for congregations and parishes based on results from a survey of church attenders in four nations. The ICLS project was conducted in April and May 2001, with more than 12,000 congregations and 1.2 million worshipers participating. Each congregation invited all worshipers to complete a survey. The congregations also completed a congregational profile form, and the key leader in each congregation answered questions as well. Survey results are being used to provide individualized reports to each participating congregation and to produce books, research reports, and other resources about religious life in the twenty-first century.

The ICLS is conducted by the following agencies and people:

Australia: The National Church Life Survey (NCLS) sponsored by ANGLICARE NSW of the Anglican Church in Australia, the New South Wales Board of Mission of the Uniting Church in Australia, and the Australian Catholic Bishops Conference: Dean Drayton (convener of the ICLS steering committee), John Bellamy, Keith Castle, Howard

Dillon*, Robert Dixon, Peter Kaldor (founding director of NCLS), Ruth Powell, Tina Rendell*, and Sam Sterland

England: Churches Information for Mission (CIM): Phillip Escott, Alison Gelder*, Roger Whitehead*

New Zealand: Church Life Survey–New Zealand (CLS-NZ), a subcommittee of the Christian Research Association of New Zealand: Norman Brookes*

United States: U.S. Congregations supported by Lilly Endowment, Inc.; the Louisville Institute; and the Research Services office of the Presbyterian Church (U.S.A.): Deborah Bruce, Cynthia Woolever*, Keith Wulff*

* ICLS Steering Committee

NOTES

Introduction

1. L. Frank Baum, *The Wonderful Wizard of Oz* (New York: TAB Books, 1958).
2. W. Paul Jones, "Traveling the Yellow Brick Road," in *Weavings*, XVII: 2 (March/April 2002): 38–45.
3. Throughout this book we use the term *congregations* to refer to faith communities of all types—Catholic parishes, Protestant churches, Jewish synagogues, and others.
4. W. Wayt Gibbs, "Saving Dying Languages," in *Scientific American* (August 2002): 79–85.
5. Marcus Buckingham and Donald O. Clifton, *Now, Discover Your Strengths* (New York: Free Press, 2001).
6. Marilyn Elias, "What Makes People Happy; Psychologists Now Know," in *USA Today* (December 9, 2002): 1.
7. James Hopewell, *Congregation: Stories and Structures* (London: SCM Press, 1987).
8. Coleridge, S.T. (1817) 1951. "Biographia Littereia," in D. Stauffer, *Selected Prose and Poetry of Coleridge* (New York: Modern Library, 1951). We thank Bryan Cussen for leading us to this citation and for his writing on a "theological way of imagining." Bryan Cussen. "Pastoral Planning: A Theological Way of Imagining," a paper commissioned by the National Pastoral Planning Network (Clayton South, Victoria, Australia, October, 1999).
9. David Bayles and Ted Orland, *Art and Fear* (Consortium Book Sales and Distributors, 2001).
10. Rick Warren, *The Purpose Driven Church* (Grand Rapids: Zondervan Publishing House, 1995).
11. Christian Swartz, *Natural Church Development* (St. Charles, Ill.: ChurchSmart Resources, 2001).

12. Nicholas Evans, *The Smoke Jumper* (New York: Random House, 2001), 332.

13. Cynthia Woolever and Deborah Bruce, *A Field Guide to U.S. Congregations* (Louisville, Ky.: Westminster John Knox Press, 2002).

14. Anthony G. Pappas, *Entering the World of the Small Church* (Bethesda, Md.: Alban Institute, 2000), 25.

15. Baum, *The Wonderful Wizard of Oz,* 154.

Chapter 1

1. John Steinbeck, *The Log from the Sea of Cortez* (New York: Penguin Books, 1995; first published by Viking Press, 1951), 148.

2. Joe Hall and Sue Hammond, "What is Appreciative Inquiry?" (Thin Book Publishing Co., www.thinbook.com).

3. Israel Galindo, "The Myth of Competence," in *Congregations* (Alban Institute, winter 2003), 17.

4. David A. Roozen and C. Kirk Hadaway (eds.), *Church and Denominational Growth* (Nashville: Abingdon Press, 1993).

5. See the Conclusion (Figure 11.1) for a summary of how much American congregations differ on each of the ten strengths we identified in our research.

6. The results reported are based on logistic regression analysis. Logistic regression allows for a binary dependent variable (e.g., congregations scoring in the top 20% on the strength index vs. congregations scoring in the lower 80% on the strength index). The factors listed are statistically significant at the 0.05 level and are shown in order of importance (i.e., their ranking reflects the relative importance of the regressors in the same way as beta values do). The set of factors that predict whether a congregation's strength score will be in the top 20% of all congregations may *not* be exactly the same factors that predict congregational strength scores for the average congregation.

7. Larry Selden and Geoffrey Colvin, "Will This Customer Sink Your Stock?" in *Forbes Magazine* (September 30, 2002), 127–32.

8. To increase readability throughout the remaining chapters, liberal and mainline Protestant churches will be referred to as "mainline Protestant" churches or worshipers. In all instances, this category includes congregations that have been traditionally categorized as liberal Protestant and mainline Protestant. Appendix 3 contains the rationale and list of denominations in each category.

9. Congregations were divided into two groups based on the average age of worshipers in the congregation. Congregations with an average age *above* the national average of 52 were cate-

gorized as "older congregations." Congregations with an average age of 52 or *below* were categorized as "younger congregations." Analysis of variance was used to test for significant mean differences between the two groups on the strength index. In this instance, as for all means testing results presented in this book, differences reported are statistically significant at the 0.05 level or above.

10. Multiple regression analysis produced the results reported in this section of the chapter. All ten strength scales were included in the analysis in order to assess how each strength, in combination with other strengths, predicted numerical growth. Several congregational characteristics were used as control variables: denominational family (as dummy variables); size, average worshiper age and average worshiper income; and percentage of female worshipers. We also controlled for local population growth using data from the U.S. Census. (See the Question and Answer discussion in appendix 2 for more details on this analysis.)

11. "Illustrations," *Pulpit & Study Helps*, June 1993, 12.

12. Frederick Buechner, "Faith and Fiction," in *Going on Faith: Writing as a Spiritual Quest* (New York: Marlowe & Co., 1999), 51.

Chapter 2

1. Buechner, "Faith and Fiction."

2. Woolever and Bruce, *Field Guide to U.S. Congregations*, 73.

3. See the Conclusion (Figure 11.1) for a summary of how much American congregations differ on each of the ten strengths we identified in our research.

4. Woolever and Bruce, *Field Guide to U.S. Congregations*, 61.

5. Ibid., 32.

6. The results reported are based on logistic regression analysis. See chap. 1, note 6.

7. For this analysis, congregations were divided into two groups based on the average age of worshipers in congregations. Because the average age in American congregations is fairly old (52) when compared to the average age in the U.S. population (44), the use of 52 as the age for classifying the two groups did not work especially well for understanding differences between congregations. (Remember that we're referring to those who are at least 15 years of age.) However, comparing congregations where the average age is 40 or less to those with older average ages also failed to yield a significant difference on the Meaningful Worship Index. While we found a statistically significant correlation between the average age of the congregation and how participants experienced worship, there wasn't a clear age at which these differences became important. One conclusion from these analyses is that younger worshipers who are regularly attending do find the services helpful and meaningful. But we have

no way of knowing how many other potential young worshipers never attended in the first place or chose not to return on a regular basis.

8. See the Question and Answer discussion in appendix 2 for more details on this analysis.
9. Adapted illustration from John Maxwell, *Leadership Wired* (January 28, 2003), 1.
10. K. Hadaway and P. Marler, "It All Depends on How You Ask the Question: Item Wording and Self-Reported Church Attendance in Three Nations" (presentation at the Society for the Scientific Study of Religion, Columbus, Ohio, October 2001).

Chapter 3

1. Penny Edgell, "It's Not Just a Matter of Time: How the Time Squeeze Affects Congregational Participation," in *Family Ministry*, vol. 15, no. 2 (summer 2001), 11–26.
2. Ibid.
3. See the Conclusion (Figure 11.1) for a summary of how much American congregations differ on each of the ten strengths we identified in the research.
4. The results reported are based on logistic regression analysis. See chap. 1, note 6.
5. Congregations were divided into two groups based on the average age of worshipers in the congregation. See chap. 1, note 9.
6. See the Question and Answer discussion in appendix 2 for more details on this analysis.

Chapter 4

1. John O'Donohue, *Anam Cara: A Book of Celtic Wisdom* (New York: HarperCollins Publishers, 1997).
2. Herb Miller, correspondence, 2002.
3. See the Conclusion (Figure 11.1) for a summary of how much American congregations differ on each of the ten strengths we identified in our research.
4. The results reported are based on logistic regression analysis. See chap. 1, note 6.
5. Alvin Toffler, *The Third Wave* (New York: William Morrow and Co., 1980), 383.
6. Congregations were divided into two groups based on the average age of worshipers in the congregation. See chap. 1, note 9.
7. See the Question and Answer discussion in appendix 2 for more details on this analysis.
8. Trey Hammond, "Another Road Home," Epiphany Sunday sermon at La Mesa Presbyterian Church, Albuquerque, New Mexico, January 5, 2003.

Chapter 5

1. See the Conclusion (Figure 11.1) for a summary of how much American congregations differ on each of the ten strengths we identified in our research.

2. The results reported are based on logistic regression analysis. See chap. 1, note 6.
3. Michael Masser and Linda Creed, "The Greatest Love of All," 1977.
4. Mary Gautier, correspondence, 2003.
5. Congregations were divided into two groups based on the average age of worshipers in the congregation. See chap. 1, note 9.
6. See the Question and Answer discussion in appendix 2 for more details on this analysis.
7. Alison Stein Wellner, *American Demographics* (June 2001), 52.
8. Christian Smith, Robert Faris, Melinda Lundquist Denton, and Mark Regnerus, "Mapping American Adolescent Subjective Religiosity and Attitudes of Alienation Toward Religion: A Research Report," in *Sociology of Religion* (spring 2003), 111–33.

Chapter 6

1. Kenneth B. Byerly, "Connecting: A Leader's Guide for Congregational Reflection Using the U.S. Congregational Life Survey" (www.uscongregations.org, 2003).
2. Woolever and Bruce, *Field Guide to U.S. Congregations*, 56.
3. Richard Southern and Robert Norton, *Cracking Your Congregation's Code* (San Francisco: Jossey-Bass, 2001), 7.
4. Woolever and Bruce, *Field Guide to U.S. Congregations*, 73.
5. See the Conclusion (Figure 11.1) for a summary of how much American congregations differ on each of the ten strengths we identified in the research.
6. The results reported are based on logistic regression analysis. See chap. 1, note 6.
7. Kevin A. Miller, "What We Have Uncommon," in *Leadership Weekly* (January 16, 2003), 2.
8. Herb Miller, *How to Build a Magnetic Church* (Nashville: Abingdon Press, 1987), 44.
9. Congregations were divided into two groups based on the average age of worshipers in the congregation. See chap. 1, note 9.
10. Woolever and Bruce, *Field Guide to U.S. Congregations*, 13.
11. See Questions and Answers in appendix 2 for more details on the analysis reported in this section.
12. Frances Hesselbein, "A Splendid Torch," in *Leader to Leader*, no. 22 (Fall 2001), 1.

Chapter 7

1. Herb Miller, *The Vital Congregation* (Nashville: Abingdon Press, 1990), 71.
2. See the Conclusion (Figure 11.1) for a summary of how much American congregations differ on each of the ten strengths we identified in our research.
3. The results reported are based on logistic regression analysis. See chap. 1, note 6.

4. Congregations were divided into two groups based on the average age of worshipers in the congregation. See chap. 1, note 9.
5. See the Question and Answer discussion in appendix 2 for more details on this analysis.
6. Howard W. Stone and James O. Duke, *How to Think Theologically* (Minneapolis: Fortress Press, 1989).

Chapter 8

1. George Bullard, "Learnings from Lake Hickory," in *Bullard Journal* (December 8, 2002), 1.
2. See the Conclusion (Figure 11.1) for a summary of how much American congregations differ on each of the ten strengths we identified in our research.
3. Woolever and Bruce, *Field Guide to U.S. Congregations,* 64–66.
4. The results reported are based on logistic regression analysis. See chap. 1, note 6.
5. Congregations were divided into two groups based on the average age of worshipers in the congregation. See chap. 1, note 9.
6. See the Question and Answer discussion in appendix 2 for more details on this analysis.
7. Marcus Borg, *The God We Never Knew* (San Francisco: Harper, 1998).

Chapter 9

1. Lance Secretan, "Spirit at Work," in *Industry Week* (October 12, 1998).
2. James M. Kouzes and Barry Z. Posner, *The Leadership Challenge* (San Francisco: Jossey-Bass Publishers, 1997), 30.
3. Because three of the four questions that comprise this strength ask about the congregation's key leader (pastor, minister, priest, rabbi, etc.), congregations without such leadership (whether due to pulpit vacancies or polity) will score lower than others on this index. See the Conclusion (Figure 11.1) for a summary of how much American congregations differ on each of the ten strengths we identified in our research.
4. The results reported are based on logistic regression analysis. See chap. 1, note 6.
5. Congregations were divided into two groups based on the average age of worshipers in the congregation. See chap. 1, note 9.
6. See the Question and Answer discussion in appendix 2 for details on this analysis.
7. Attributed to Ralph Nadar, source and date unknown.
8. Kouzes and Posner, *The Leadership Challenge,* 180.

Chapter 10

1. Pappas, *Entering the World of the Small Church,* 102.

2. *Executive Speechwriter Newsletter*, vol. 4, No. 5, 1989.
3. See the Conclusion (Figure 11.1) for a summary of how much American congregations differ on each of the ten strengths we identified in our research.
4. The results reported are based on logistic regression analysis. See chap. 1, note 6.
5. Congregations were divided into two groups based on the average age of worshipers in the congregation. See chap. 1, note 9.
6. See Questions and Answers in appendix 2 for more details about the analysis in this section.

Conclusion

1. A confession we share with William Zinsser (ed.), *Going On Faith* (New York: Marlowe & Co., 1999), 4.
2. John C. Sawhill, "The State of the Planet" in *National Geographic* (September 2002), 102–15.
3. Jeffrey Pfeffer and Robert I. Sutton, *The Knowing-Doing Gap* (Boston: Harvard Business School Press, 2000), 29–60.
4. Ibid.
5. Ibid., 60
6. Greg Brenneman, "Right Away and All at Once: How We Saved Continental," in *Harvard Business Review* (September-October 1998), 164.
7. Douglas Stone, Bruce Patton, and Sheila Heen, *Difficult Conversations* (New York: Penguin Books, 2000).
8. Frederick Buechner, *Wishful Thinking: A Theological ABC* (San Francisco: Harper, 1993), 120.
9. Phil Stevenson, "A Church Is Born," in Dan Reiland's *The Pastor's Coach* (February 2003, and e-mail newsletter from www.INJOY.com).
10. Pappas, *Entering the World of the Small Church*, 102.
11. Thanks to David P. Young, photographer and poet, Presbyterian Church (U.S.A.), for many conversations about who Dorothy is.
12. Psalm 138:3, 8 compiled by Nancy Schreck and Maureen Leach in *Psalms Anew* (Winona, Minn.: Saint Mary's Press, 1986).